Geometric Pattern

Coloring Book For Adults

A Huge Adult Coloring Book of 40 Theraputic Geometric Patterns for Stress Relief

Adult Coloring World

ISBN-13: 978-1522800262

ISBN-10: 1522800263

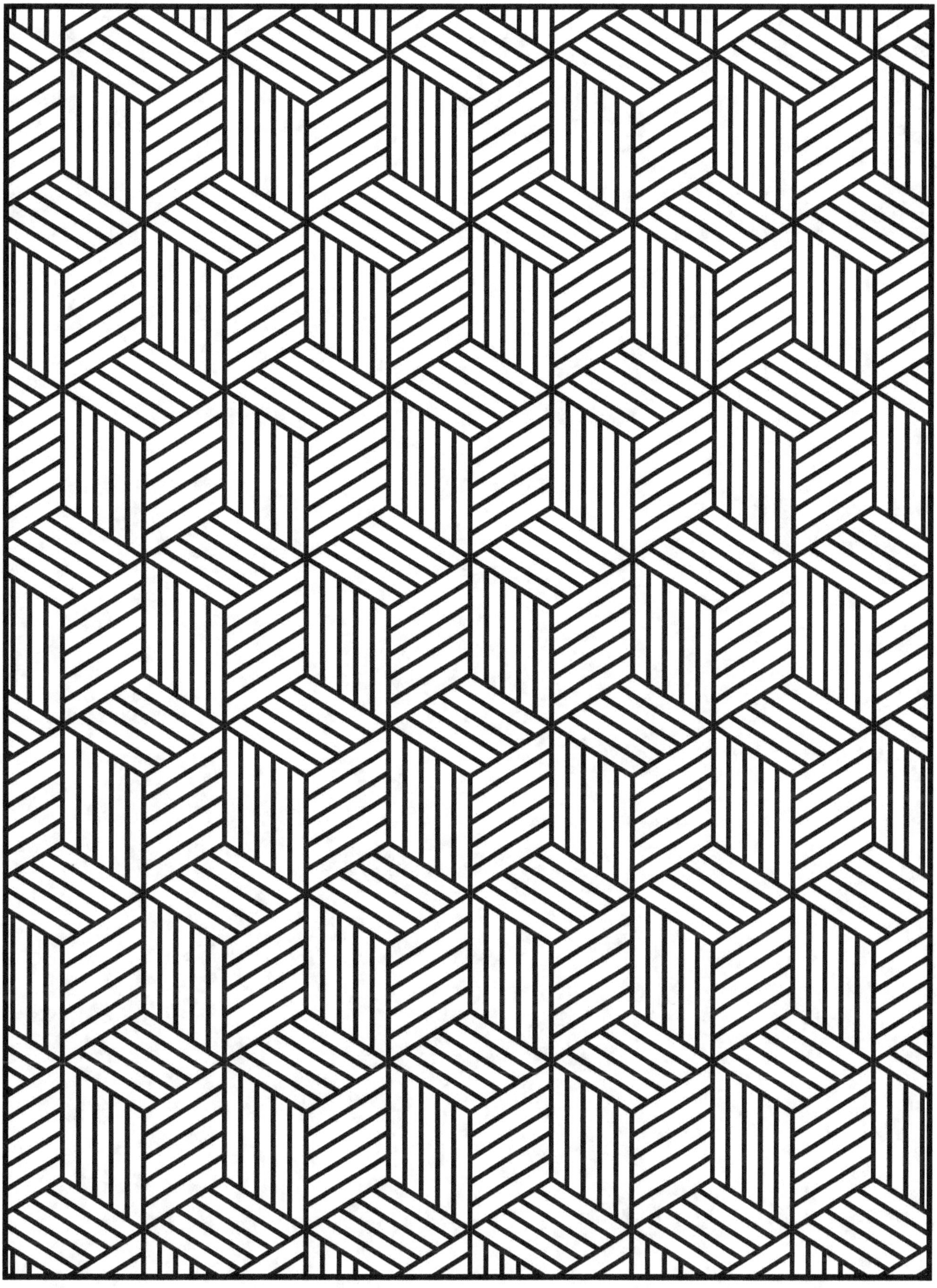

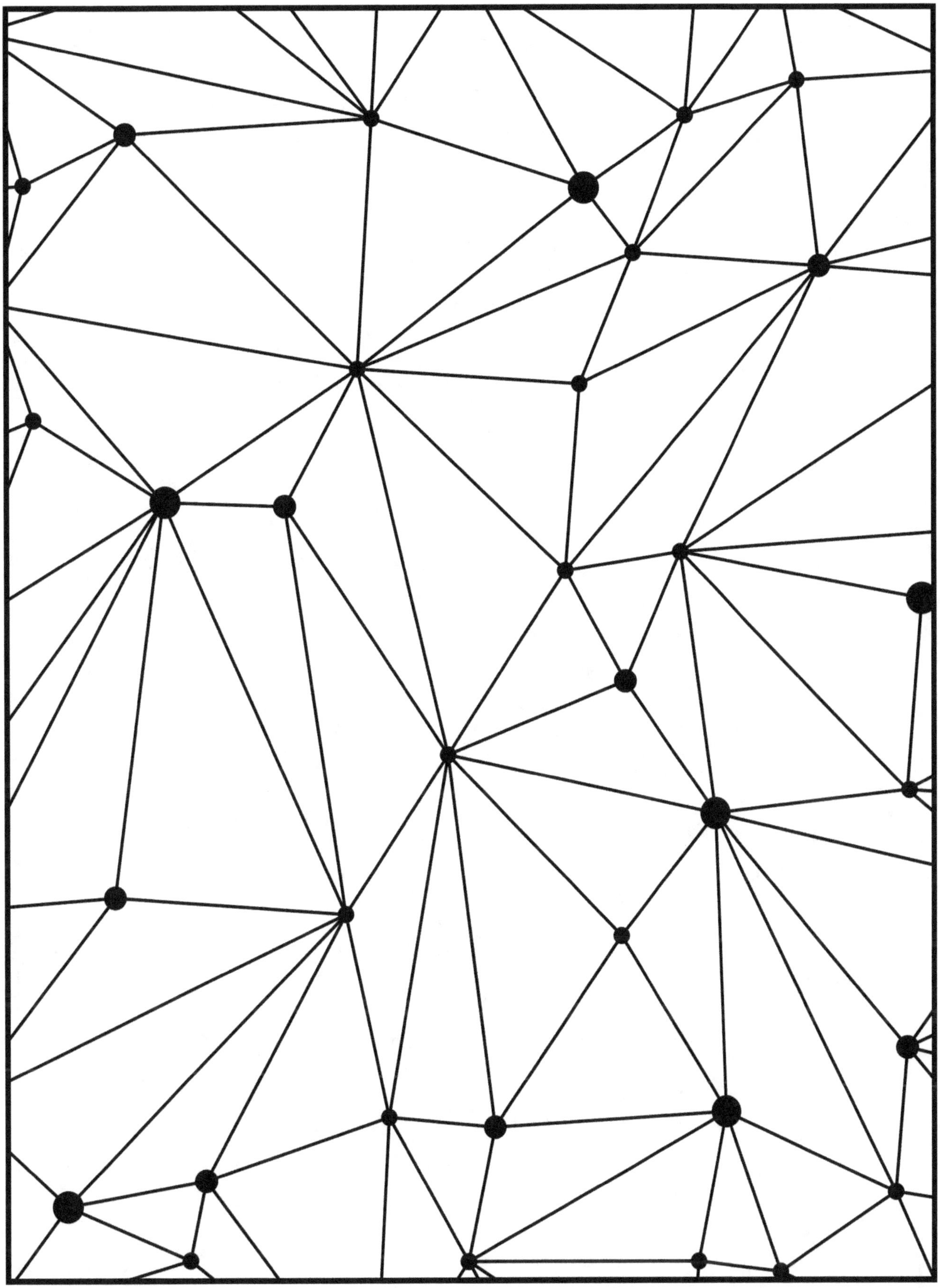

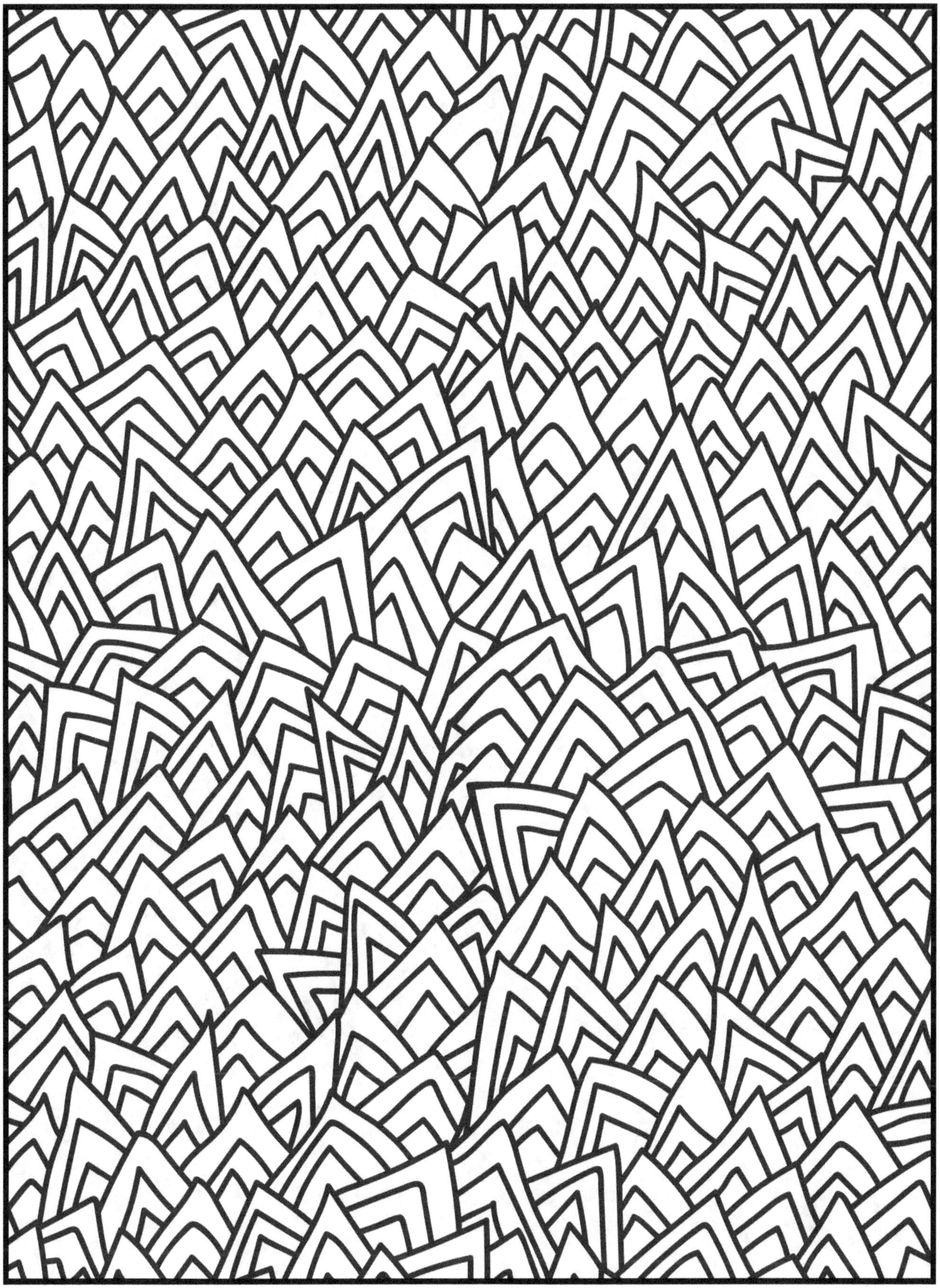

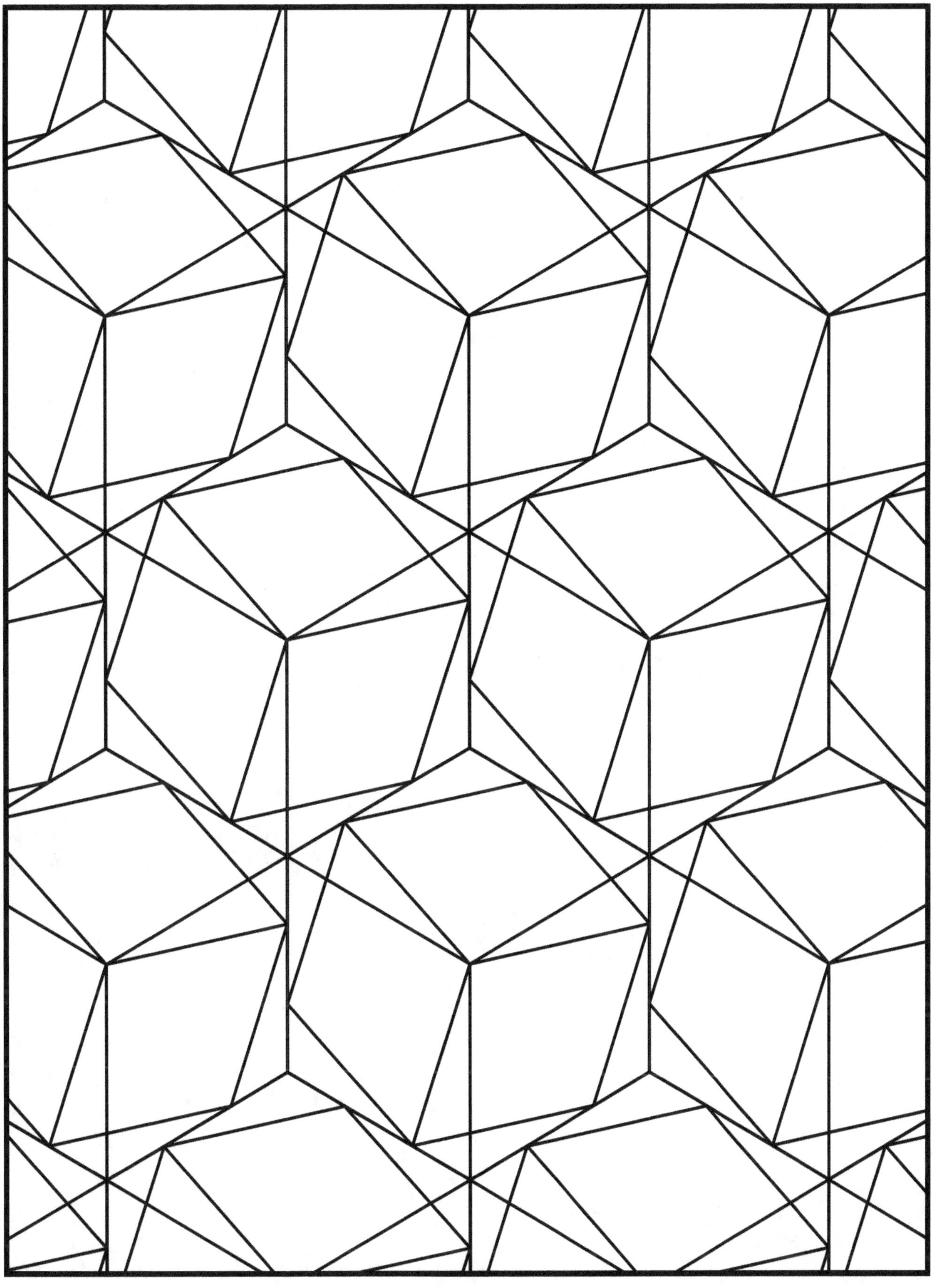

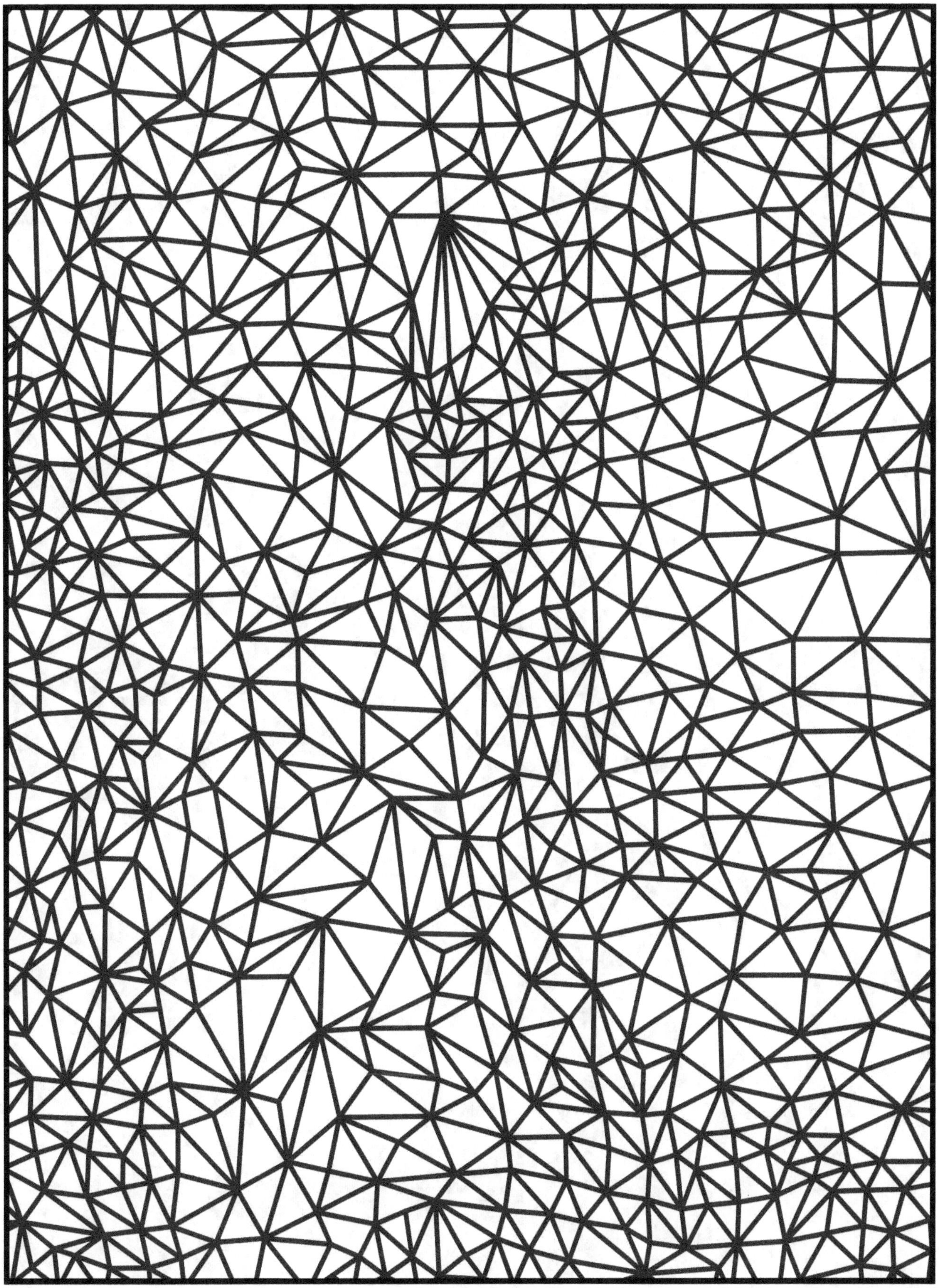

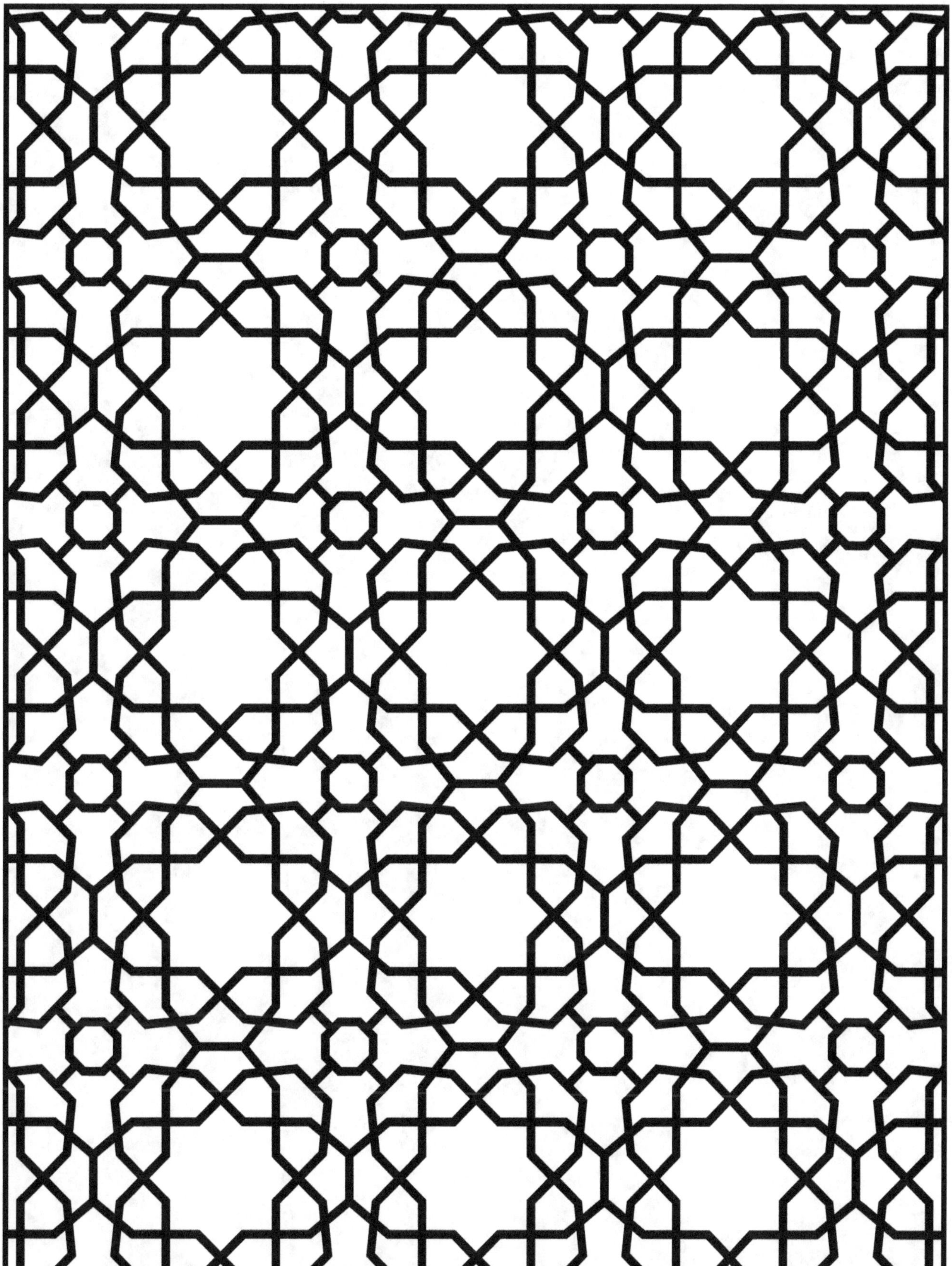

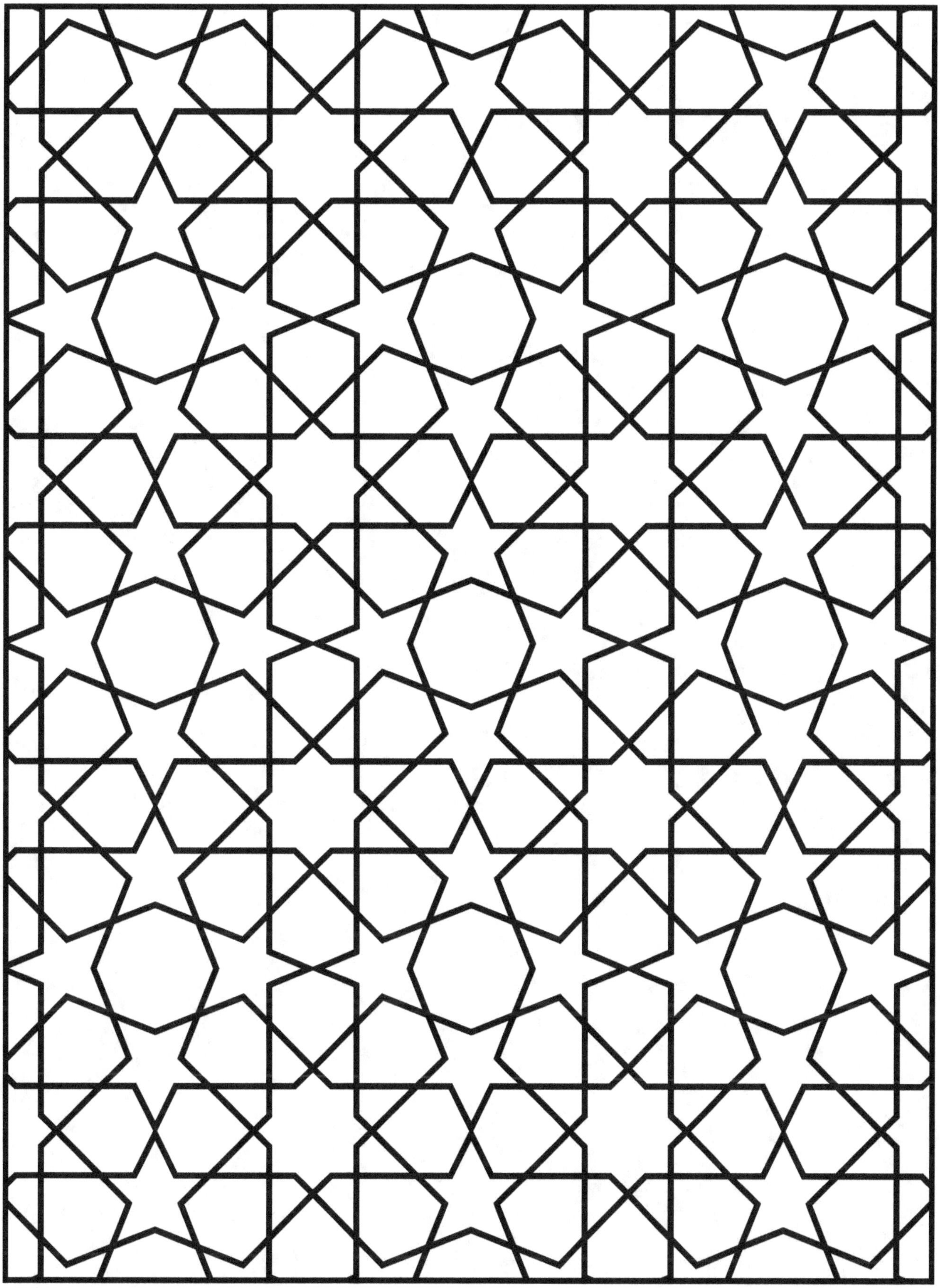

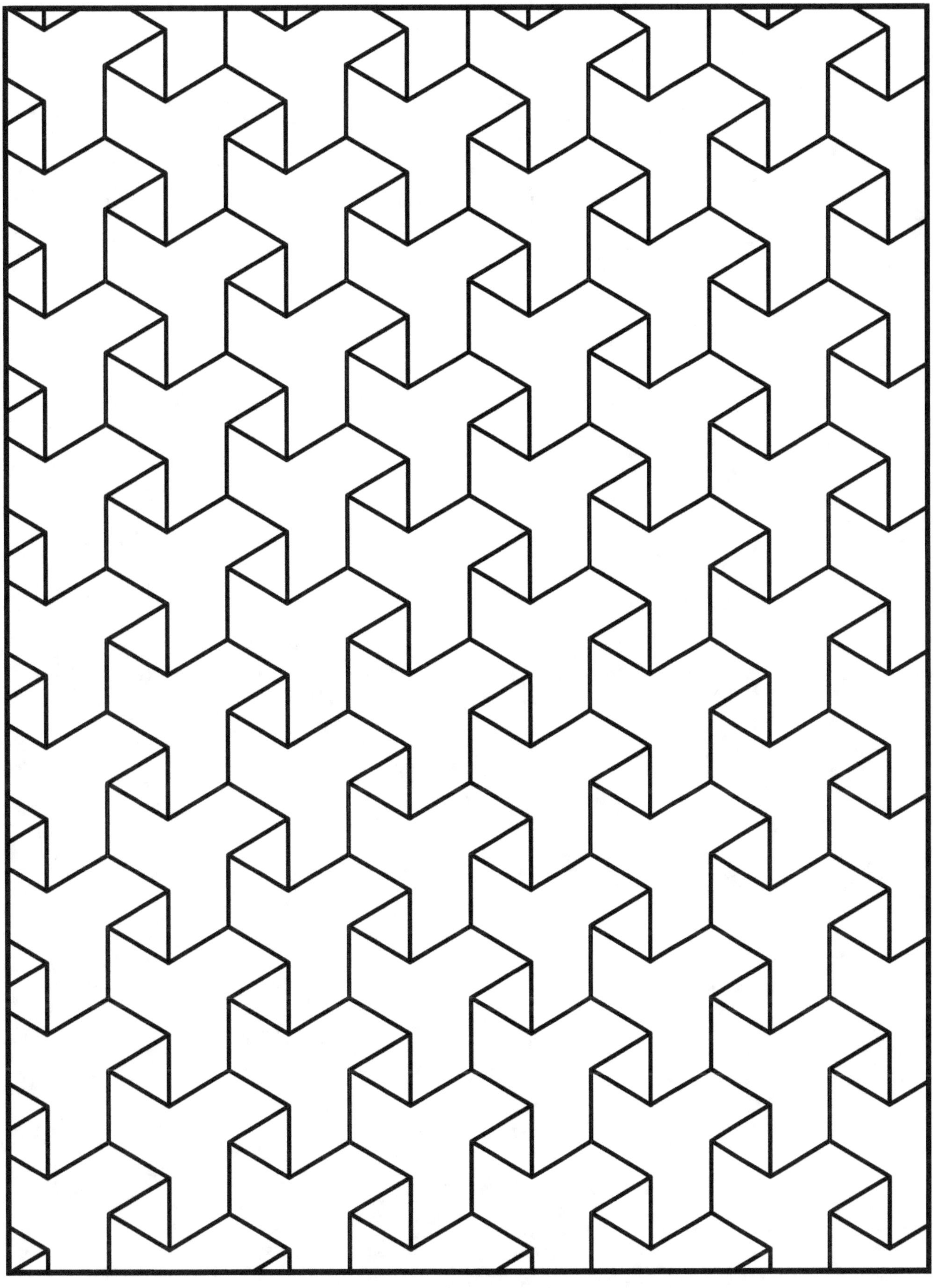

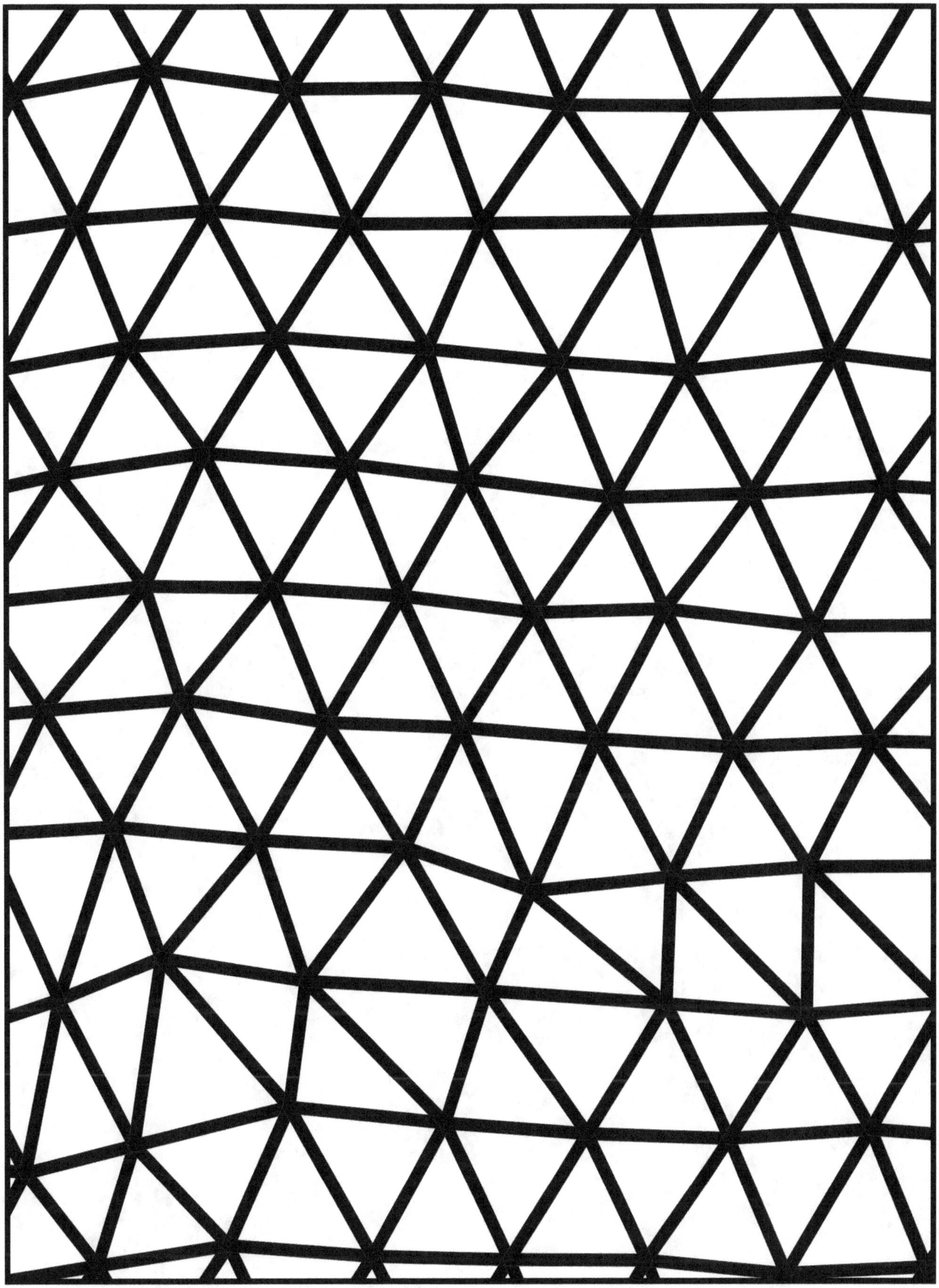

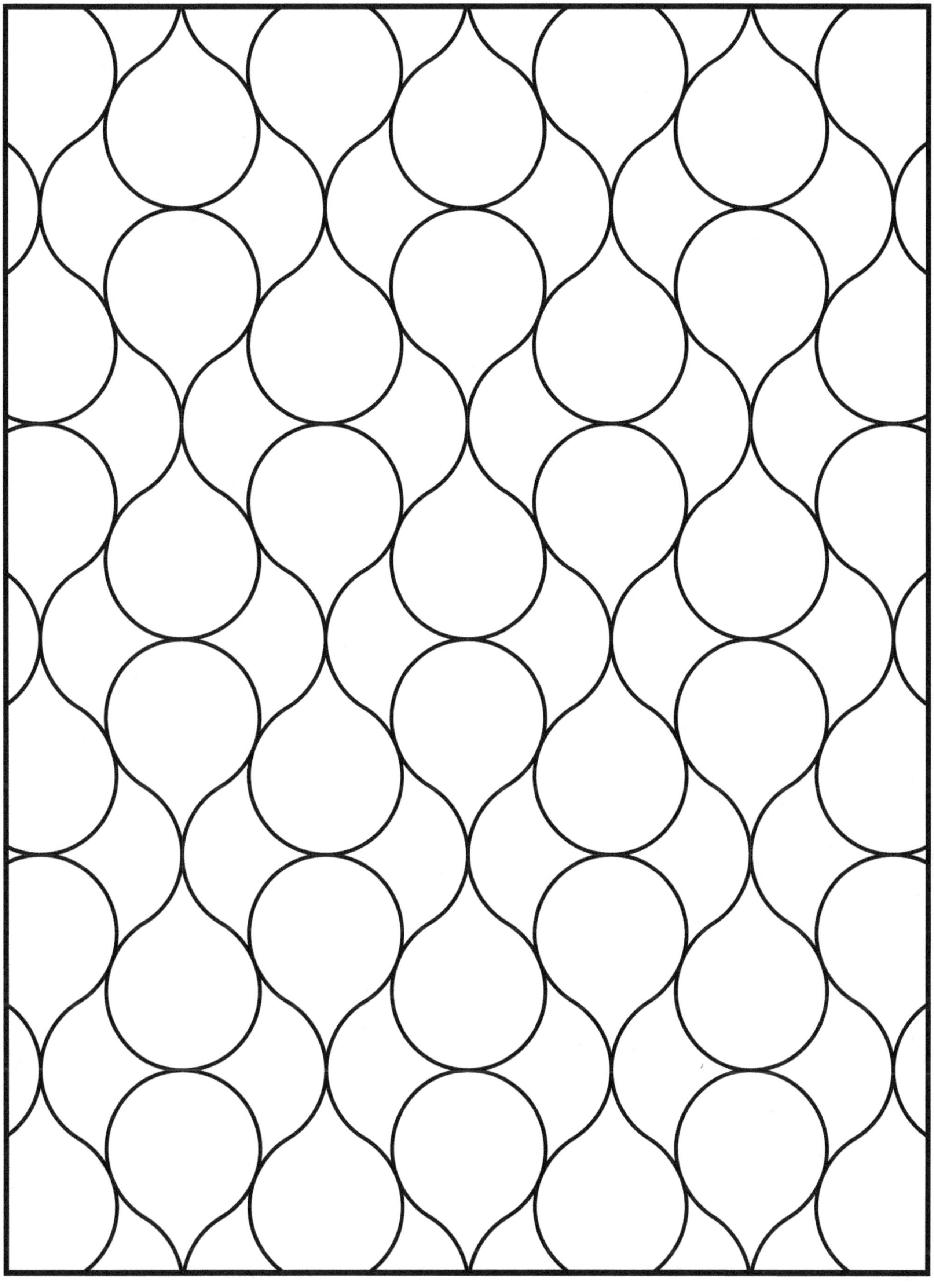

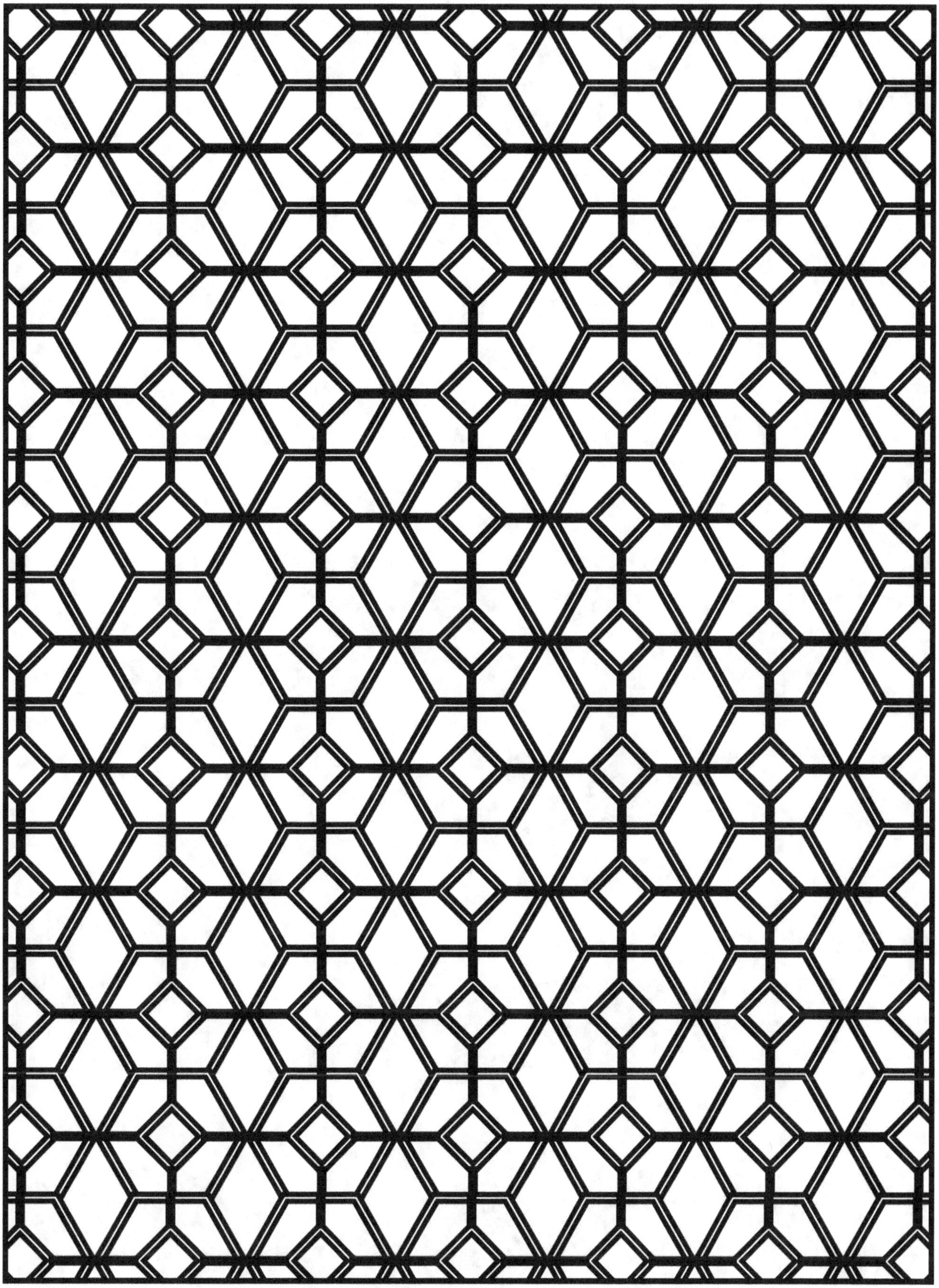

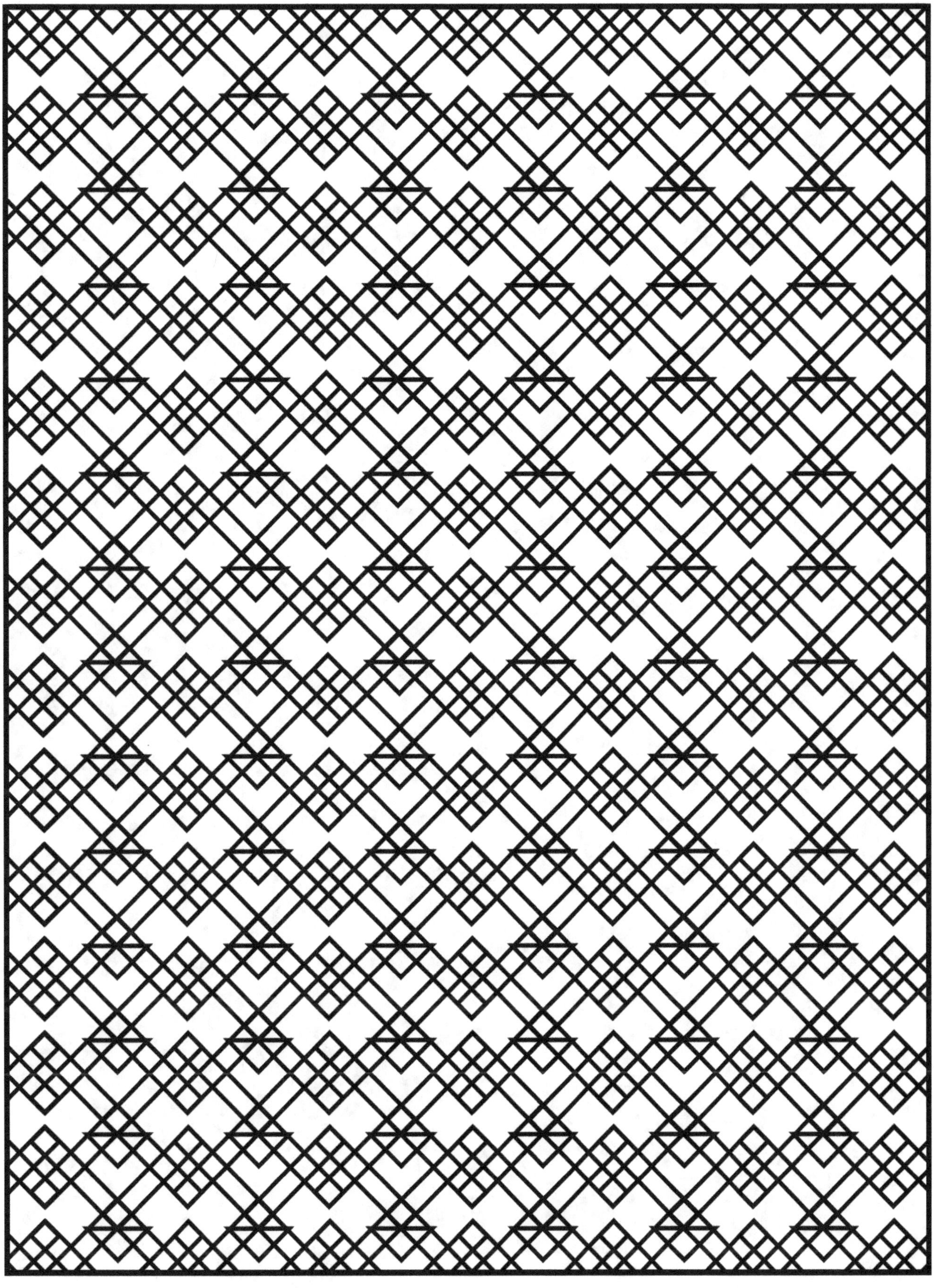

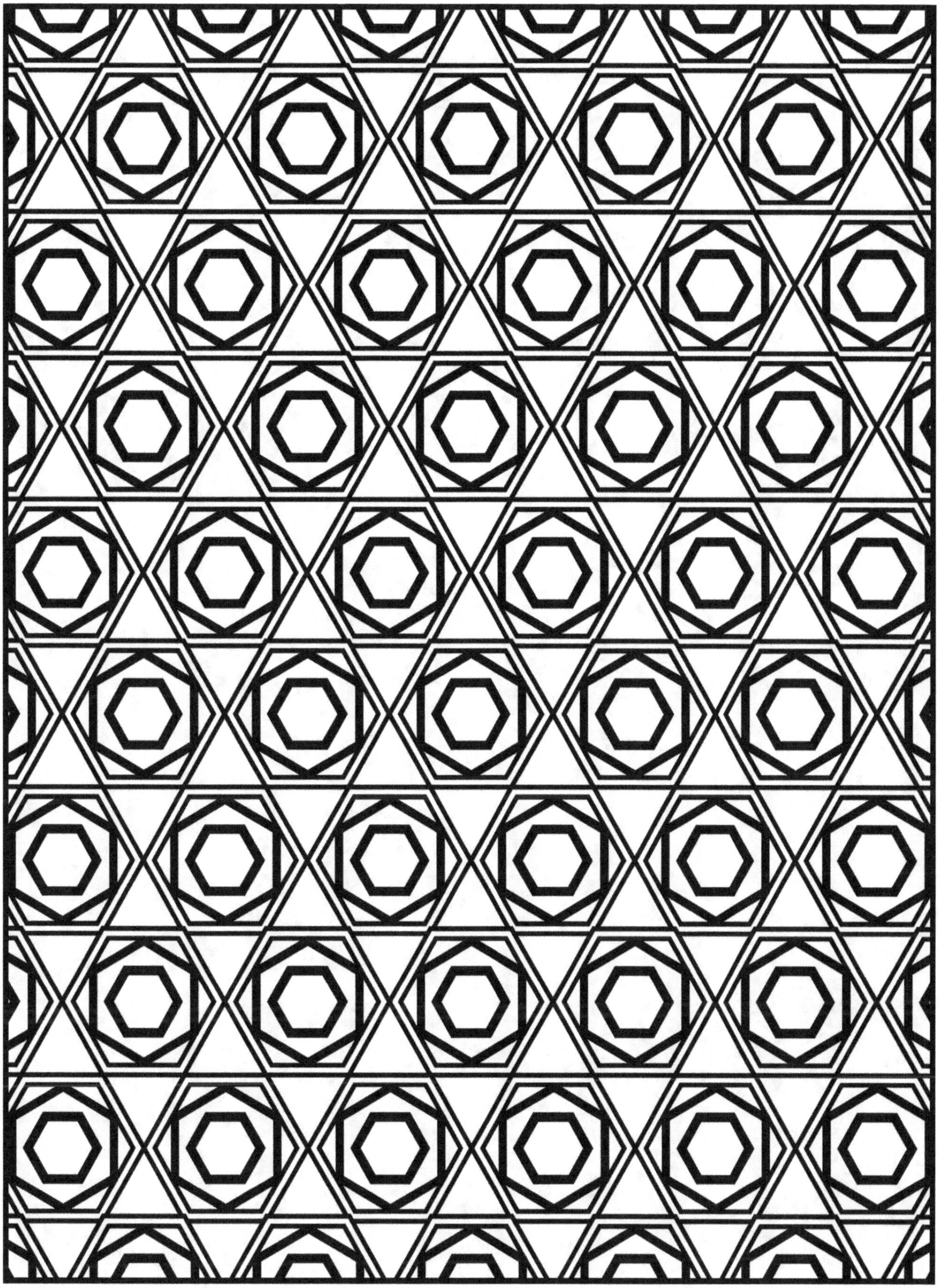

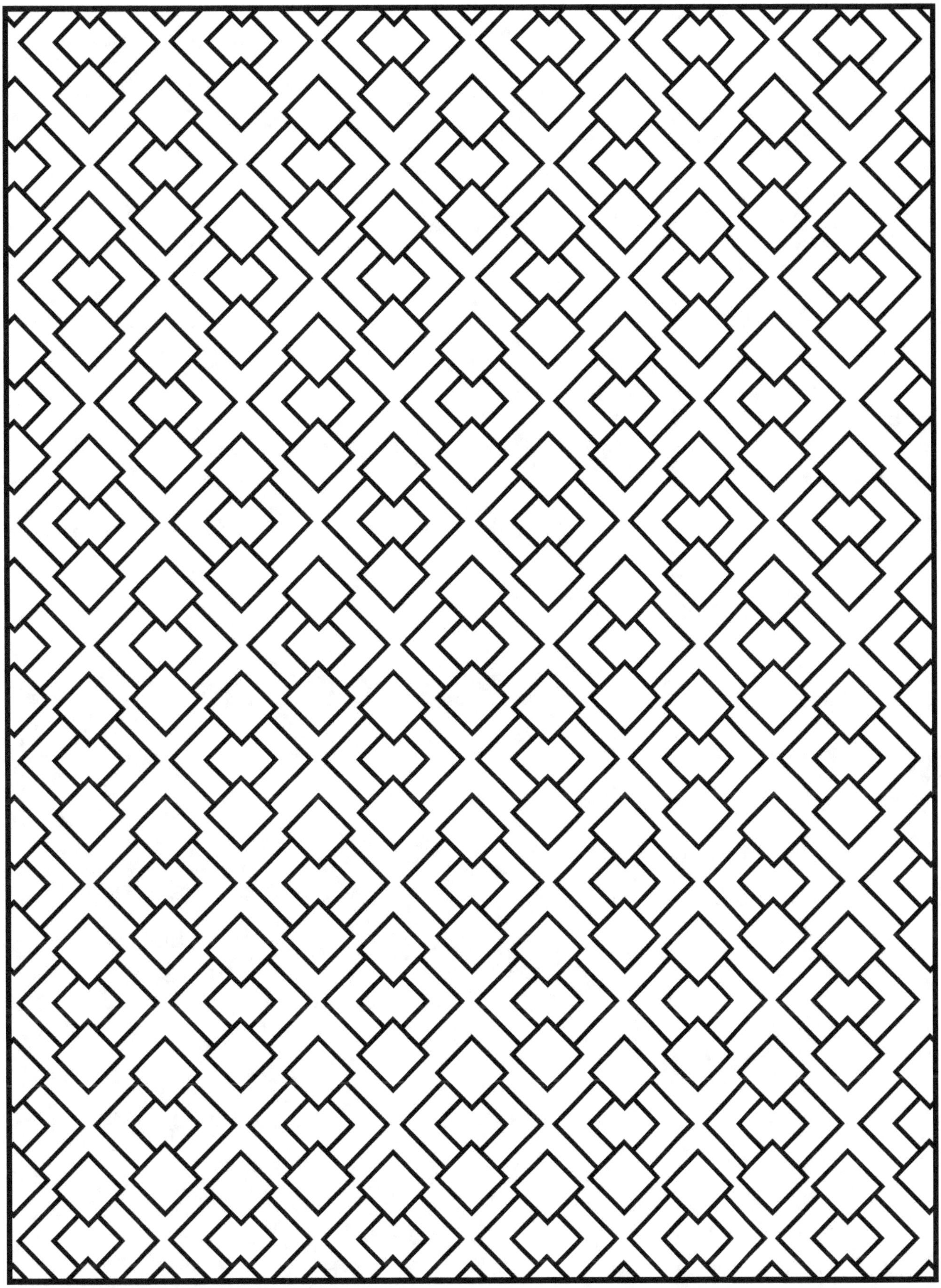

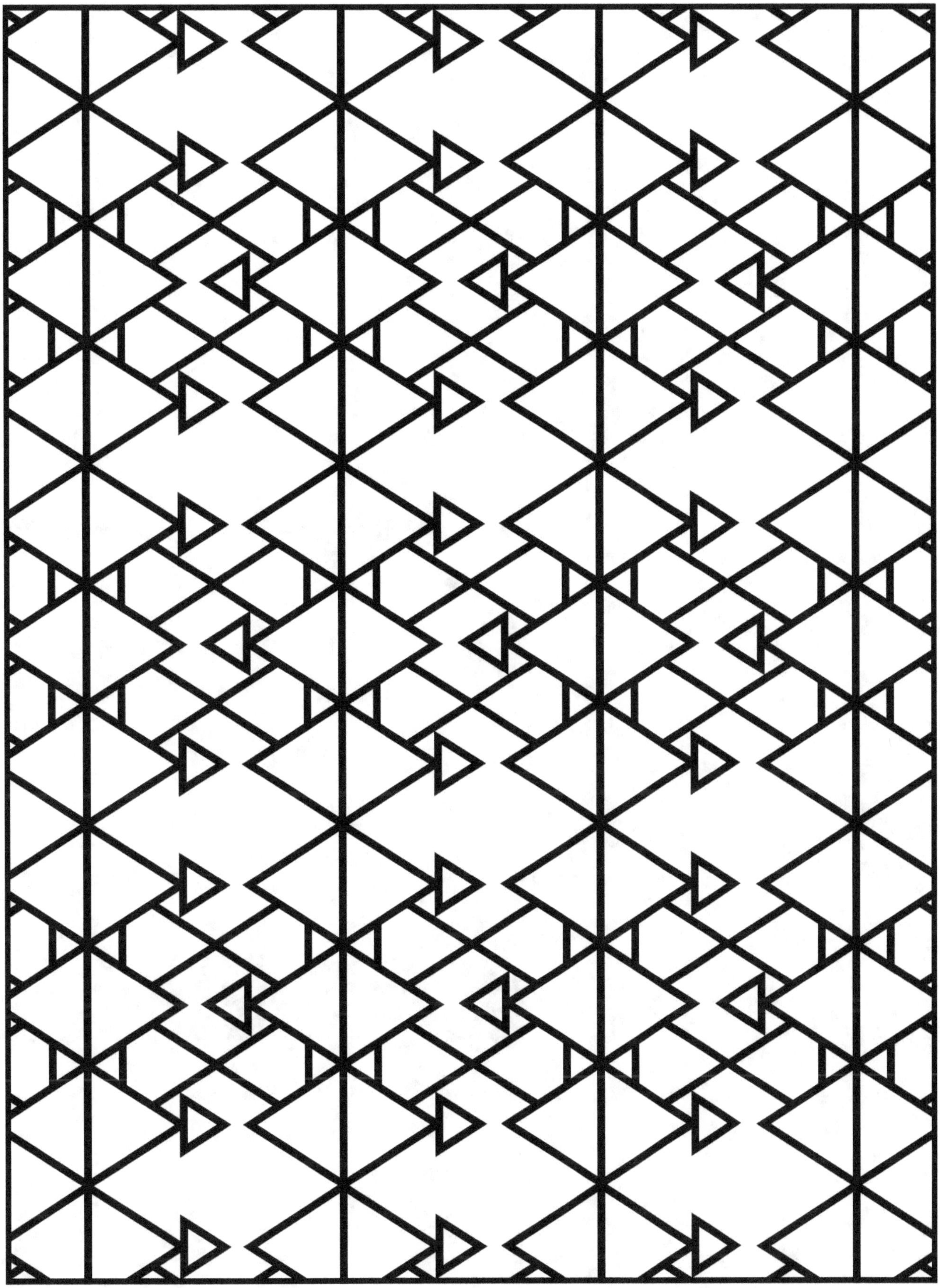

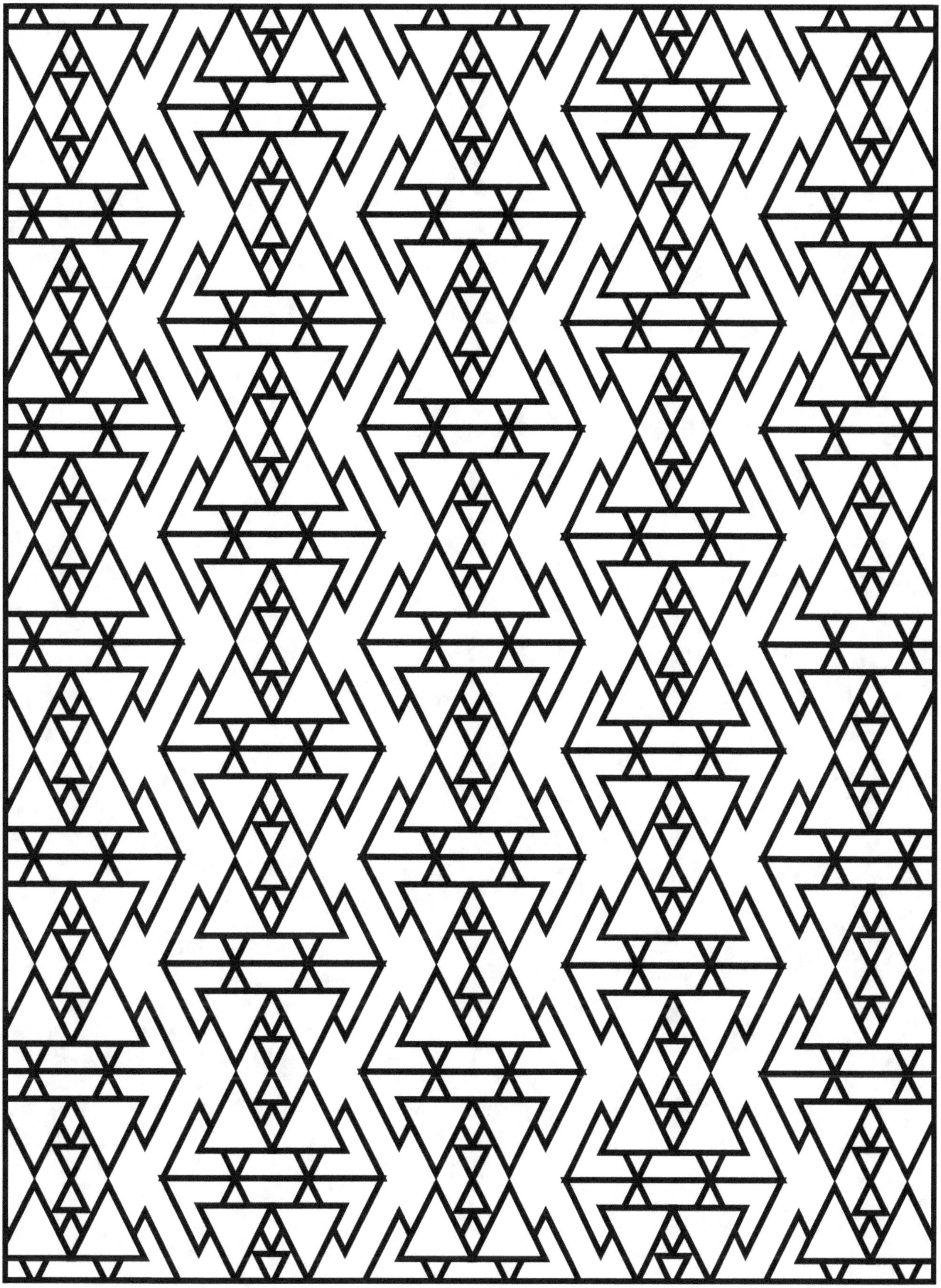

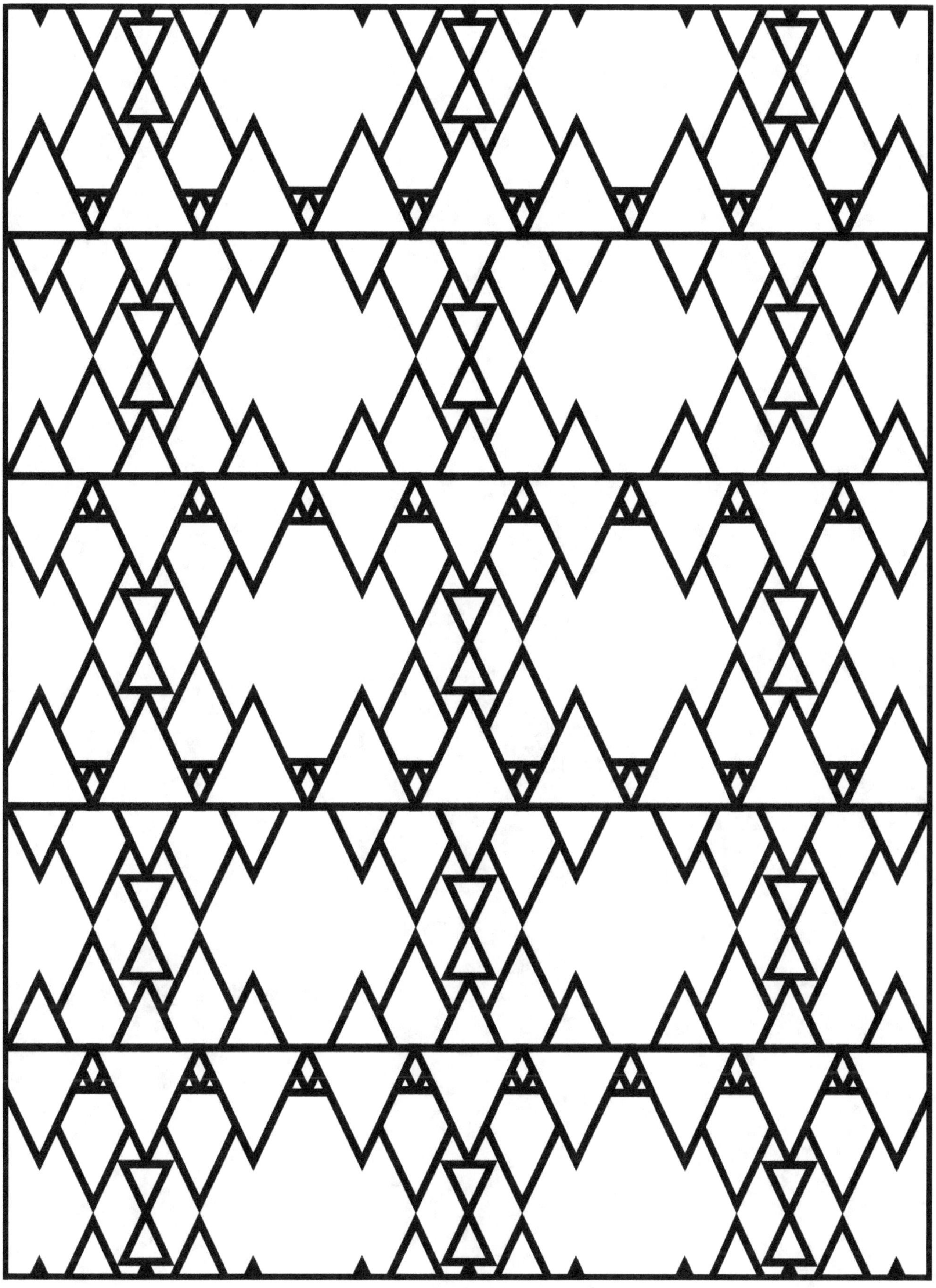

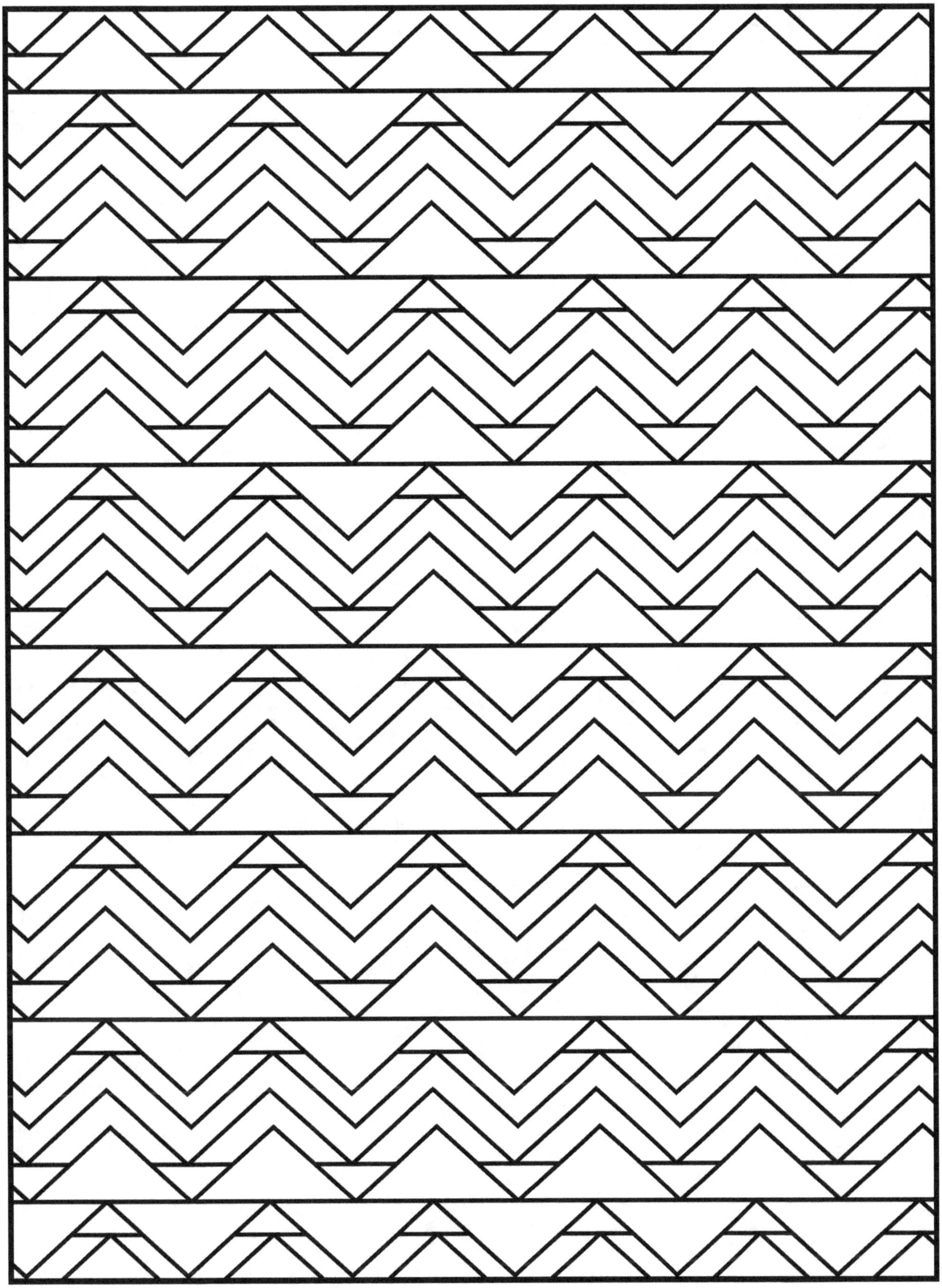

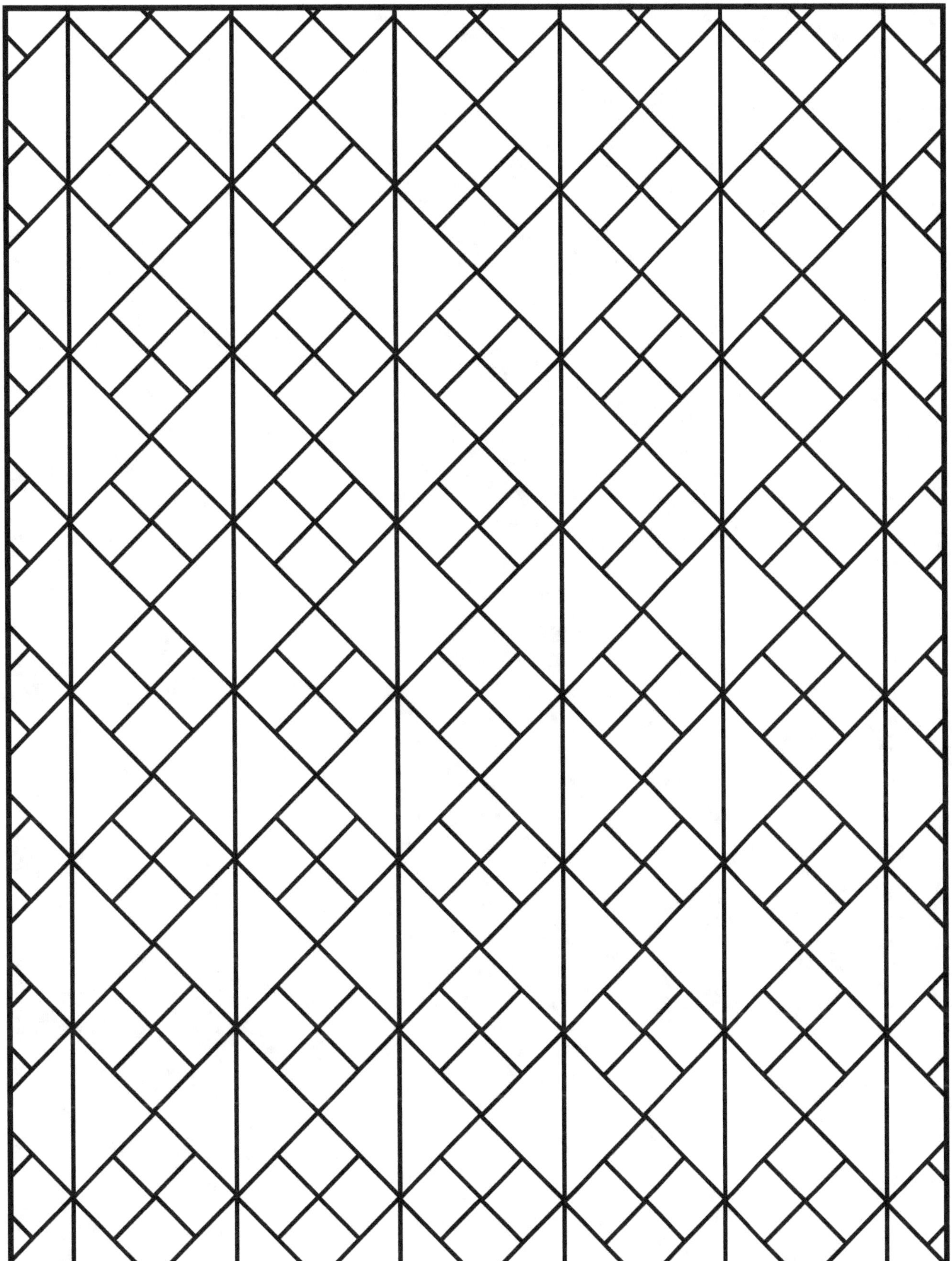

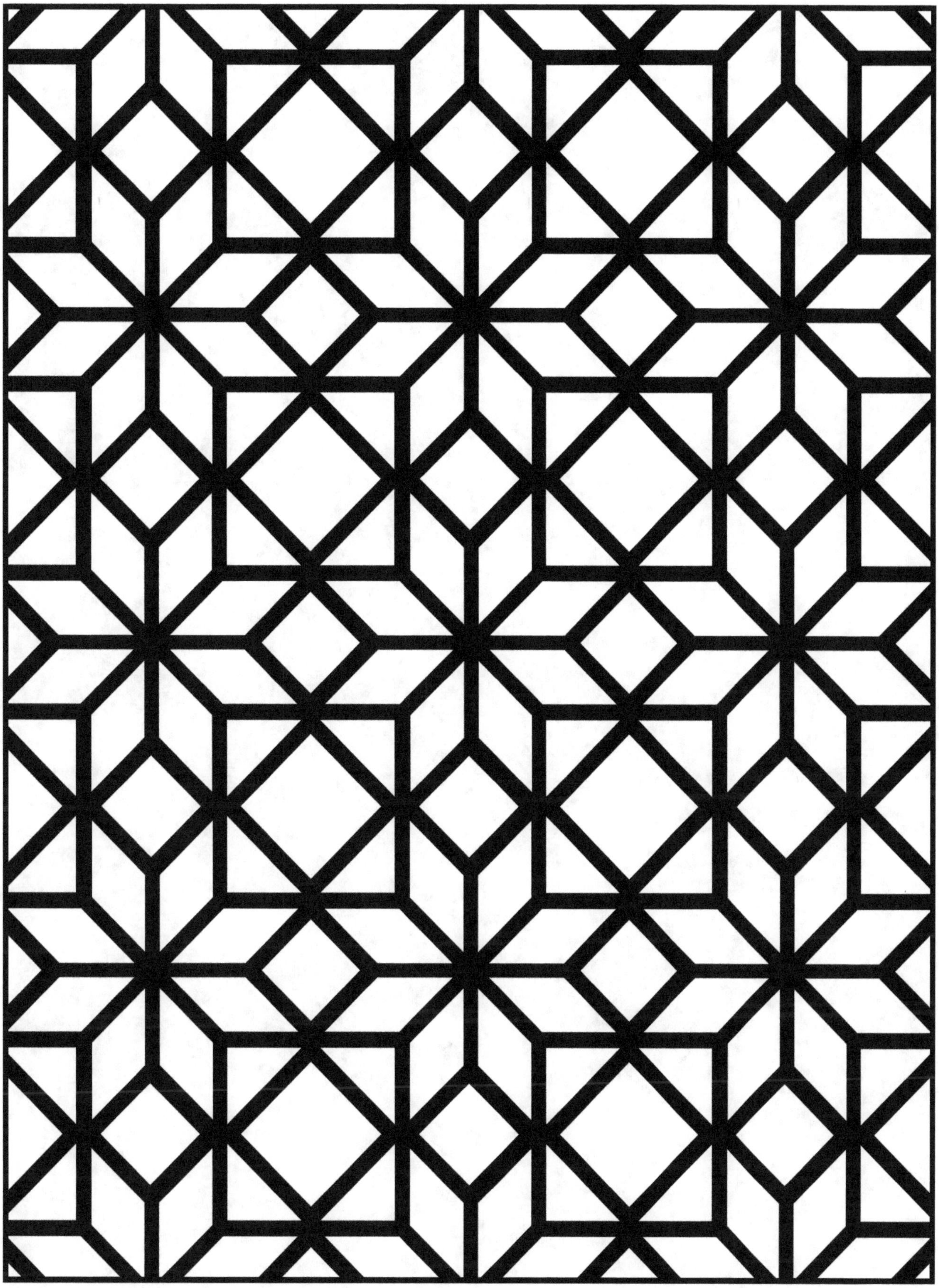

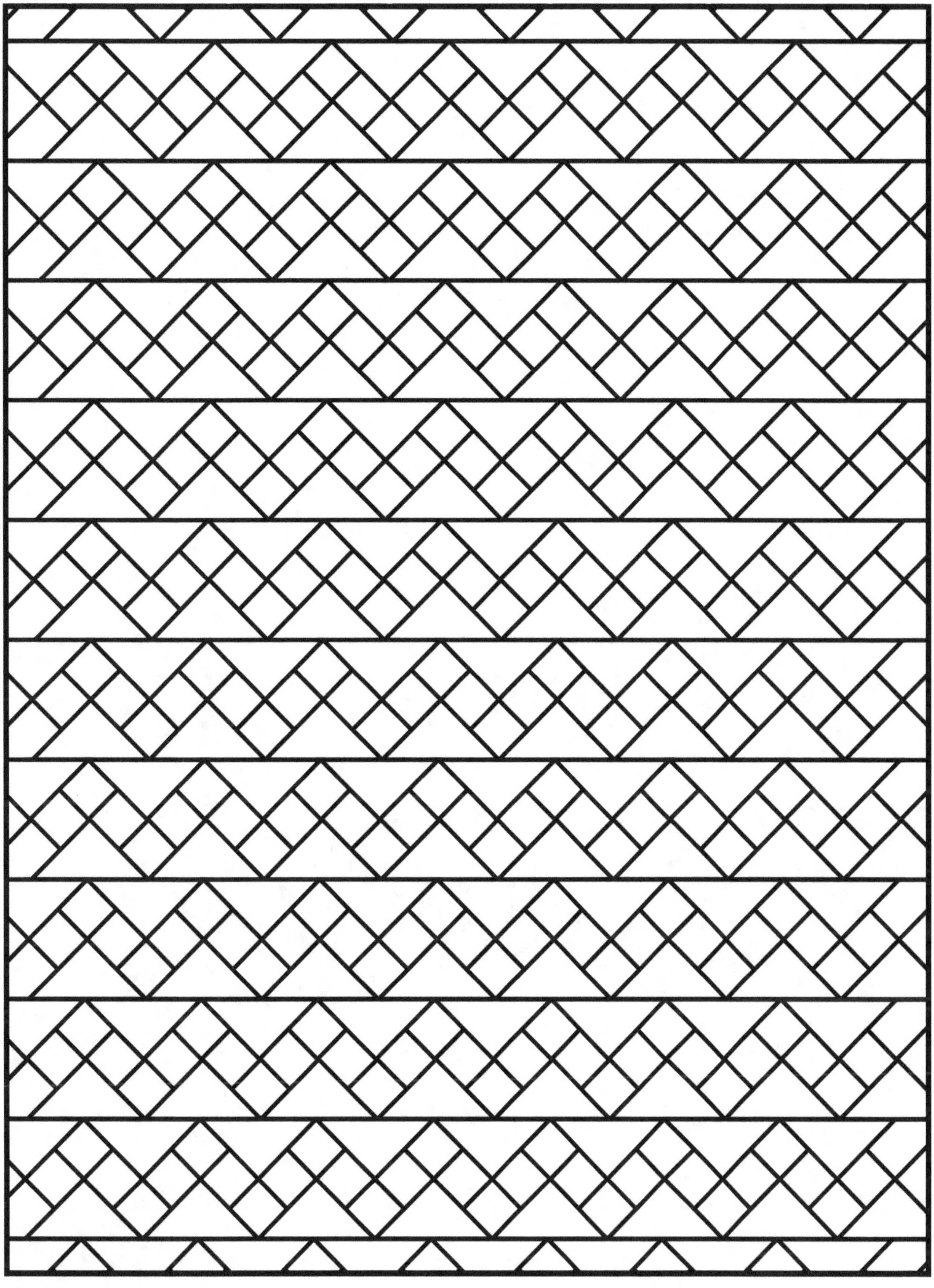

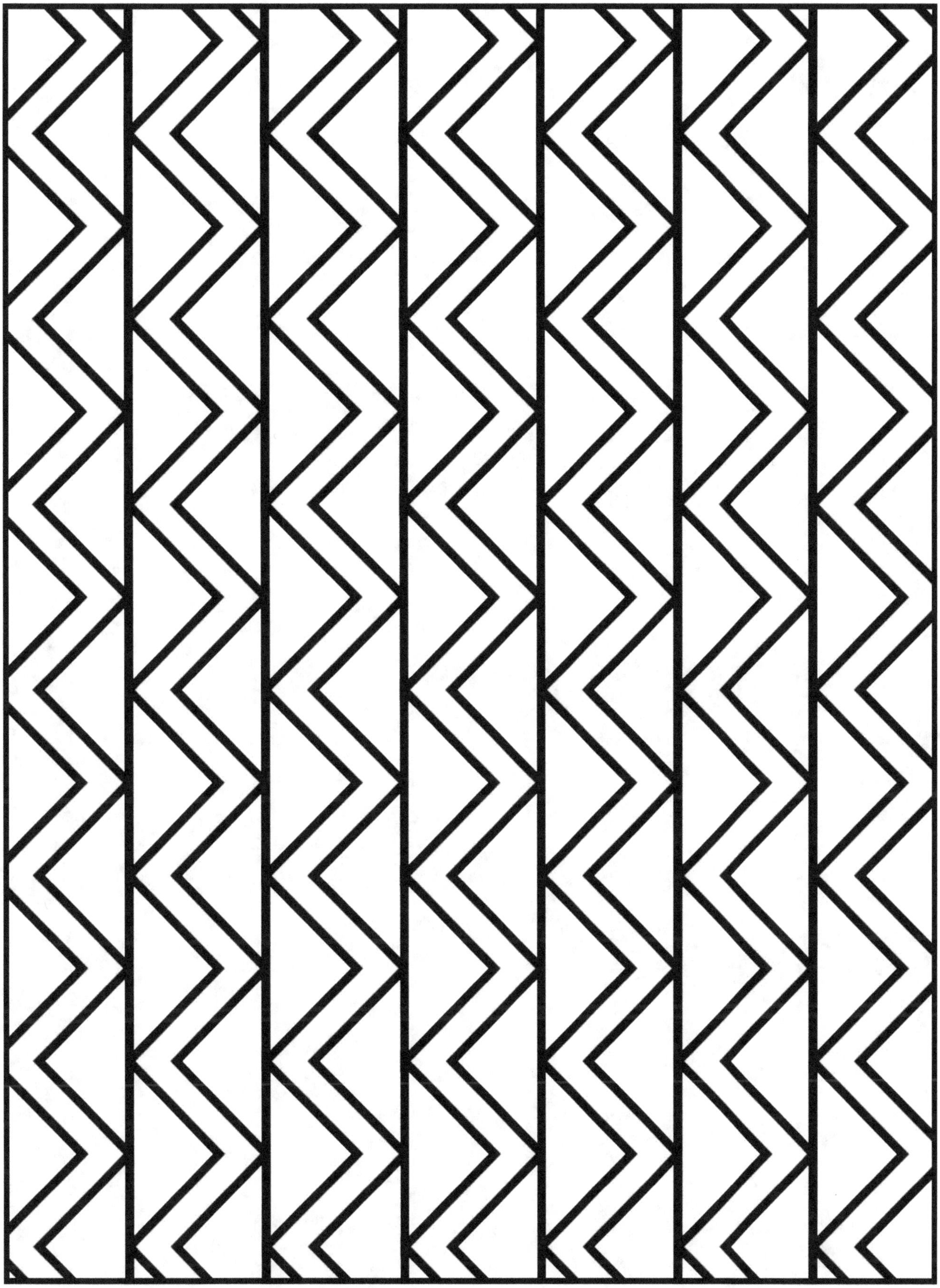

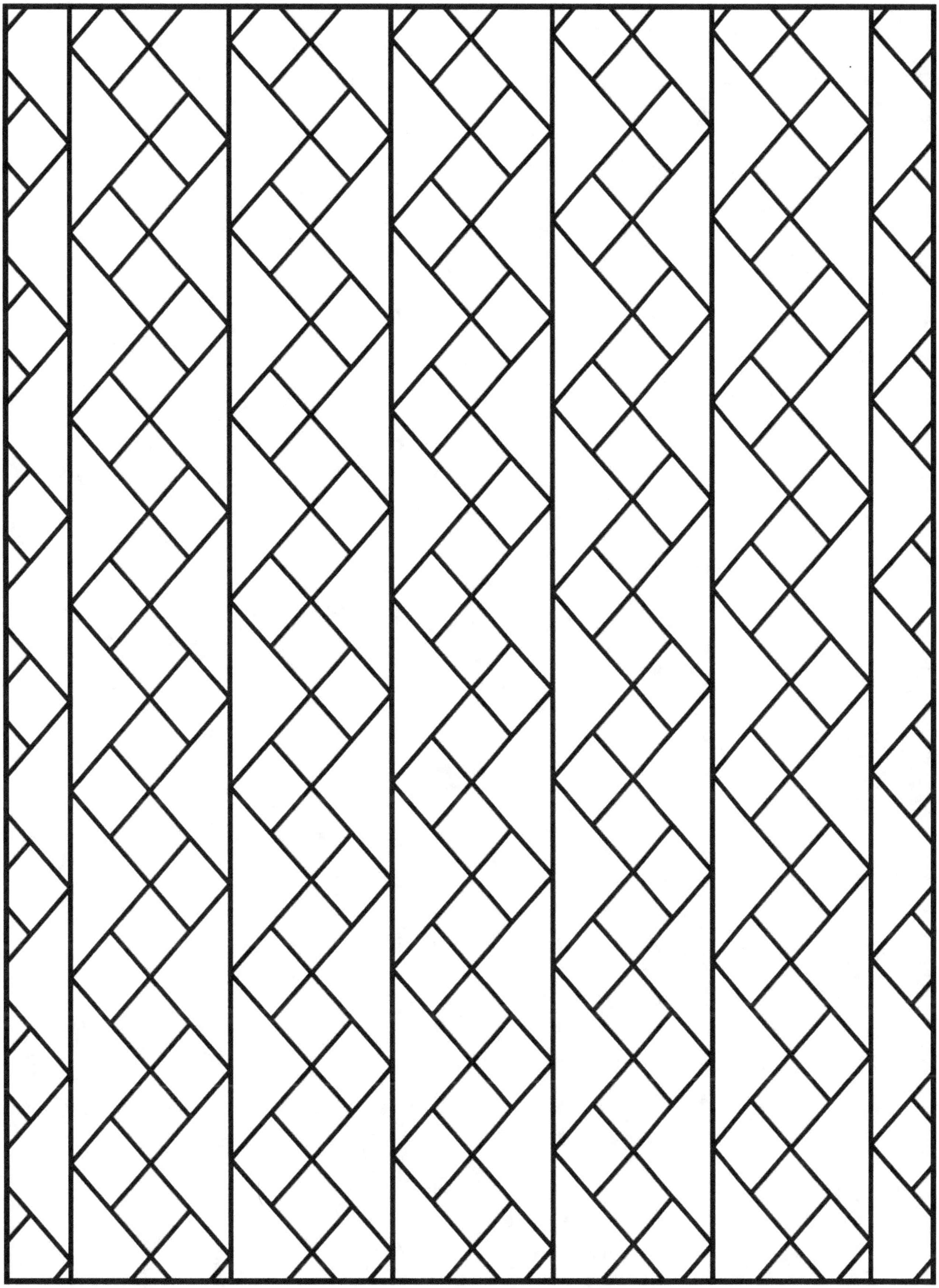

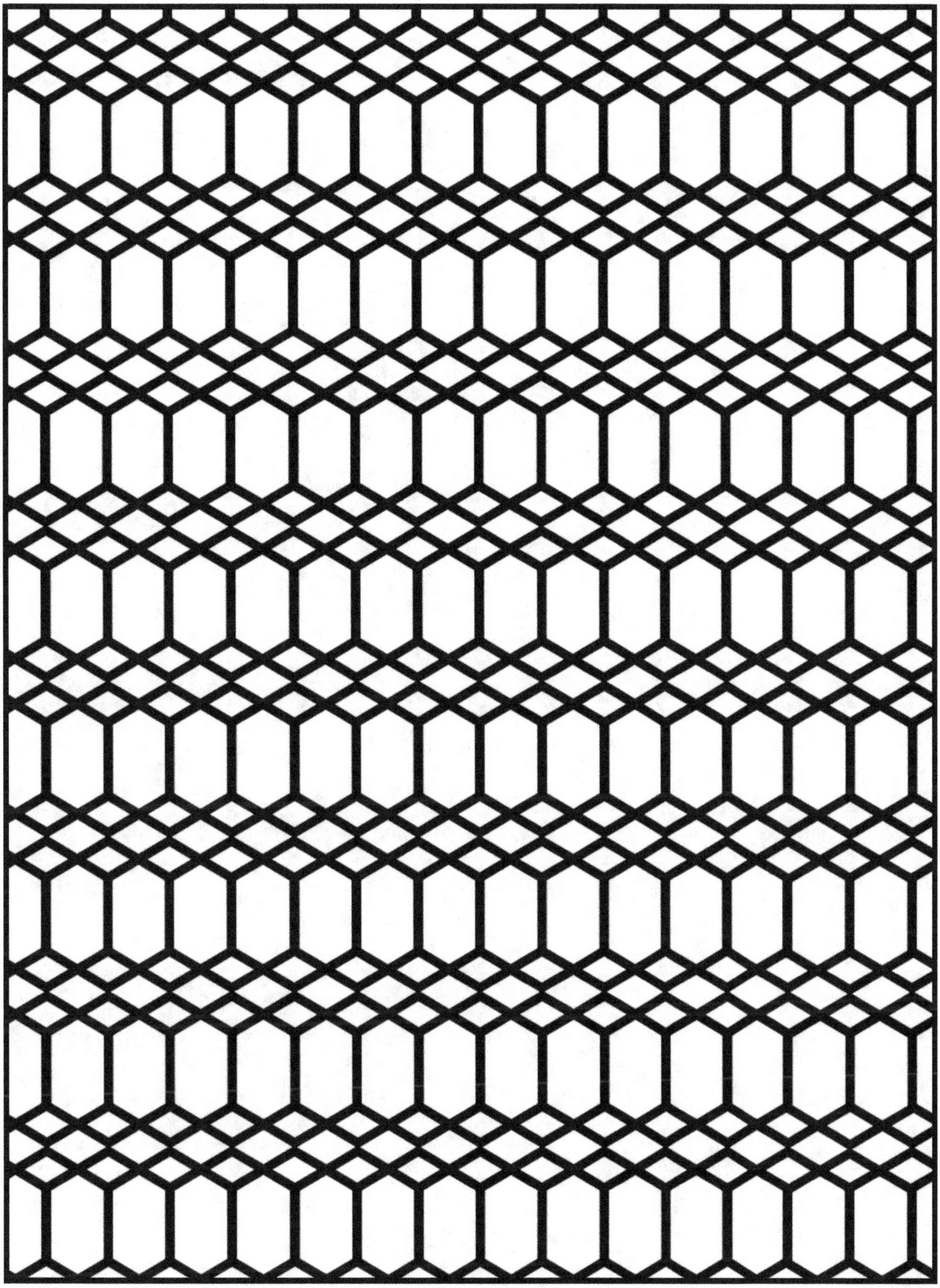

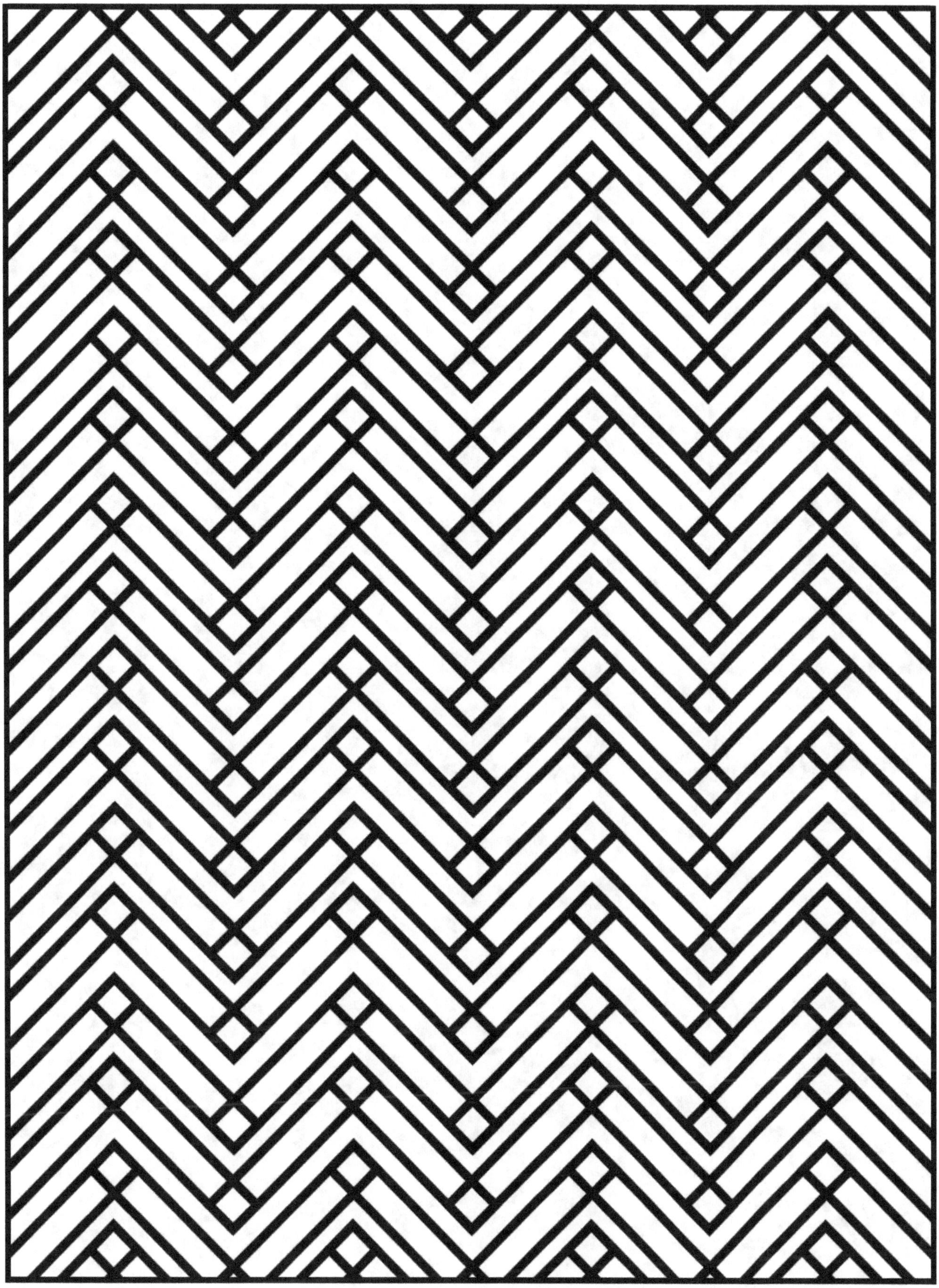

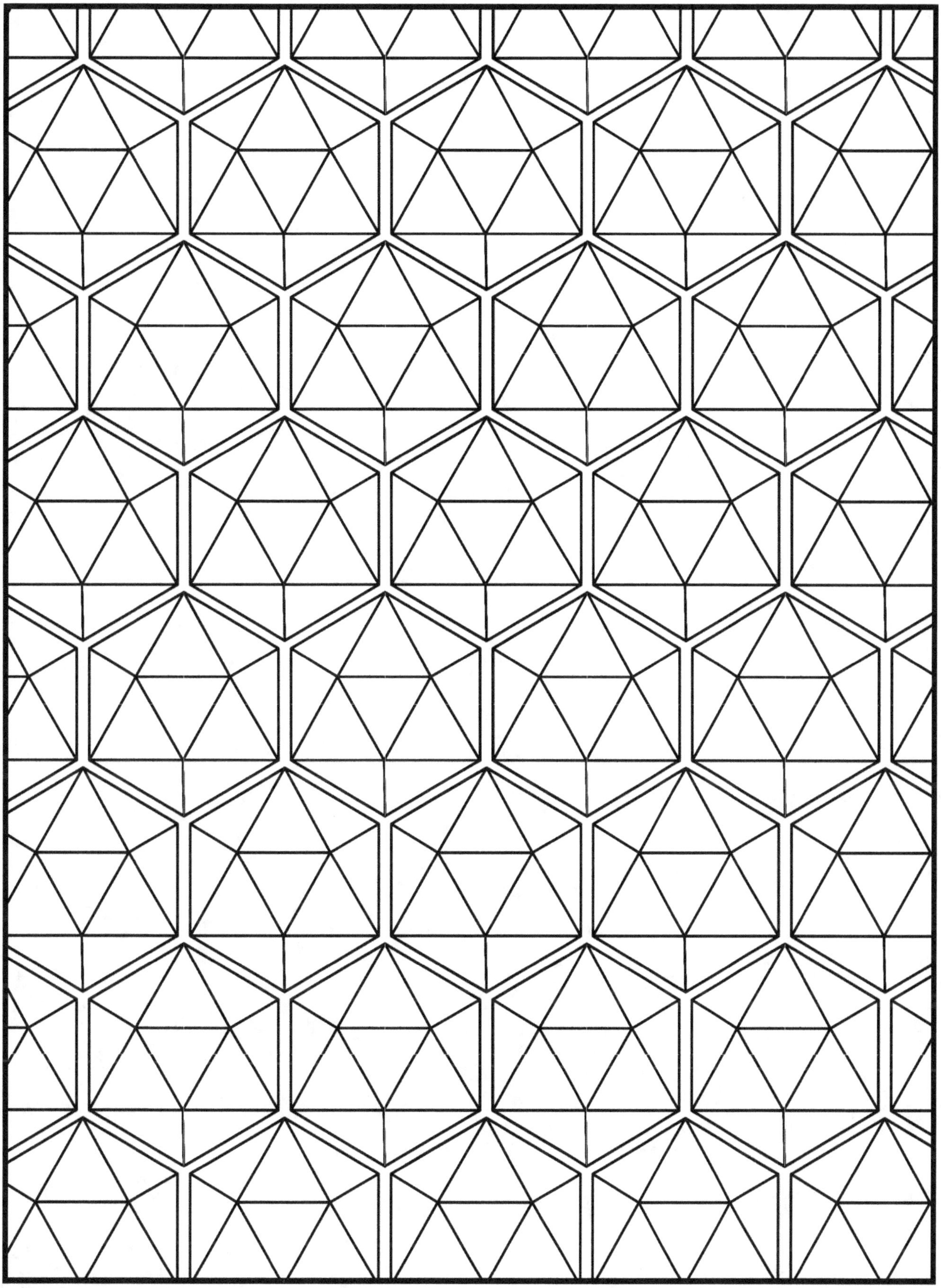

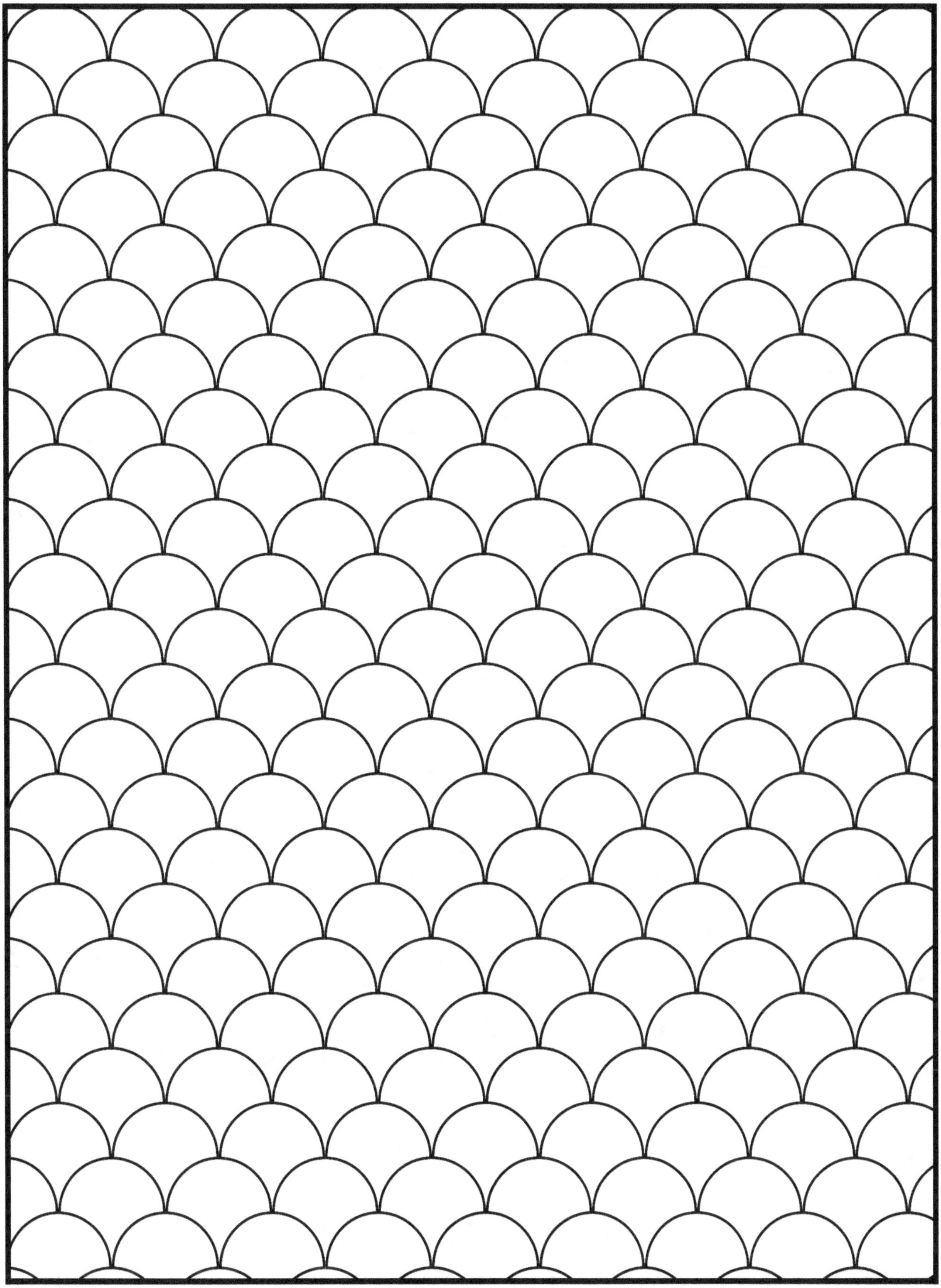

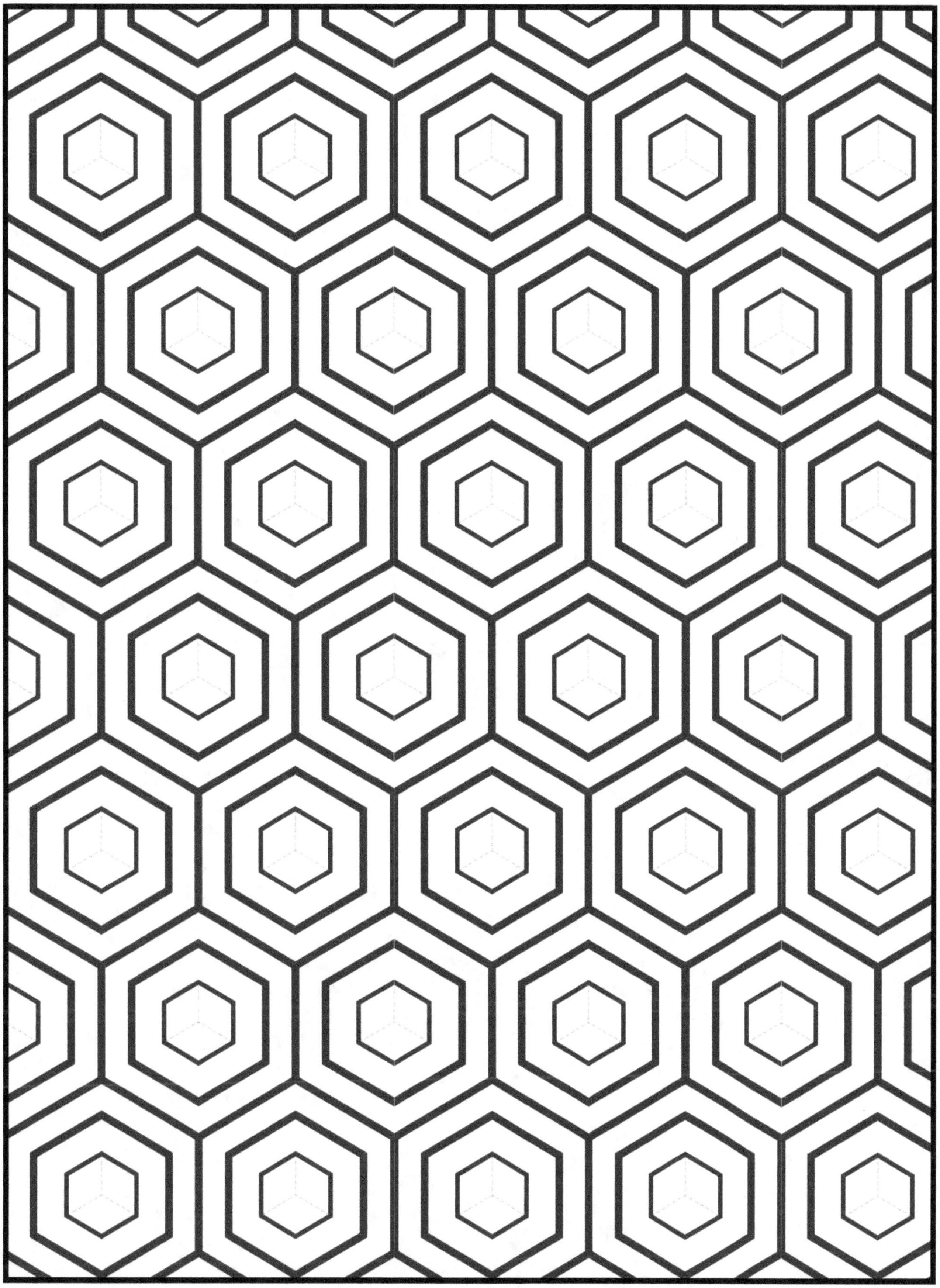

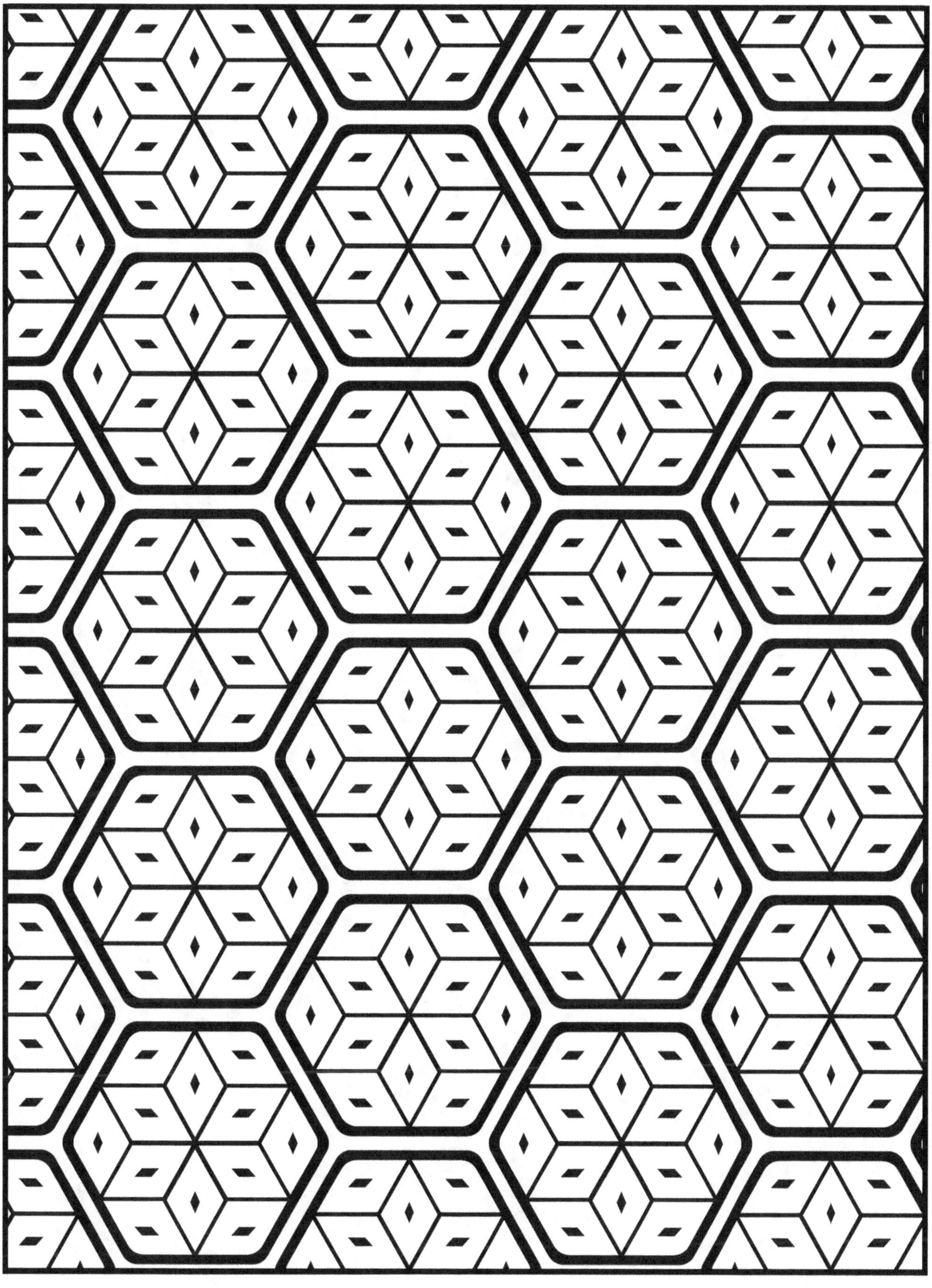

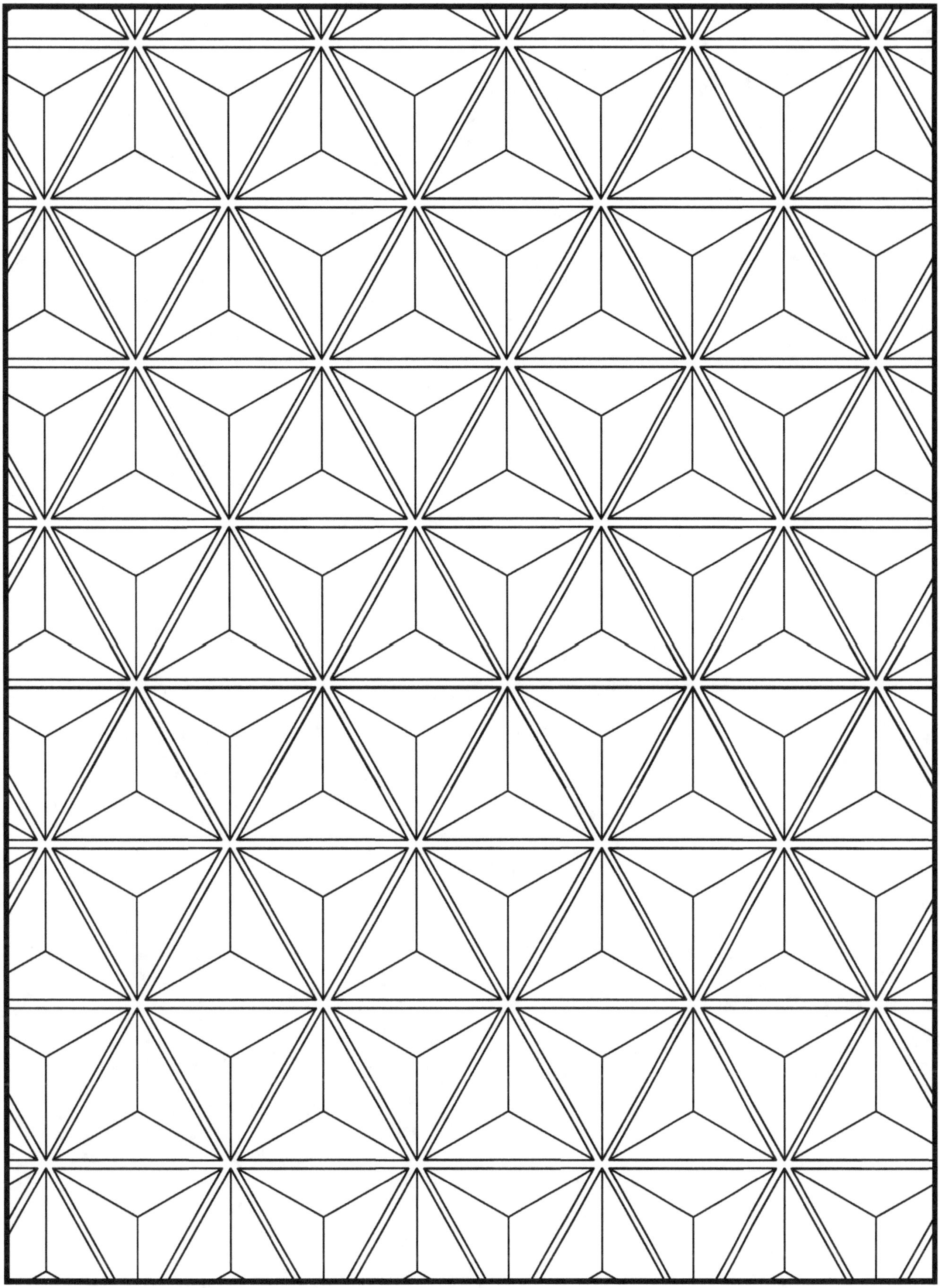

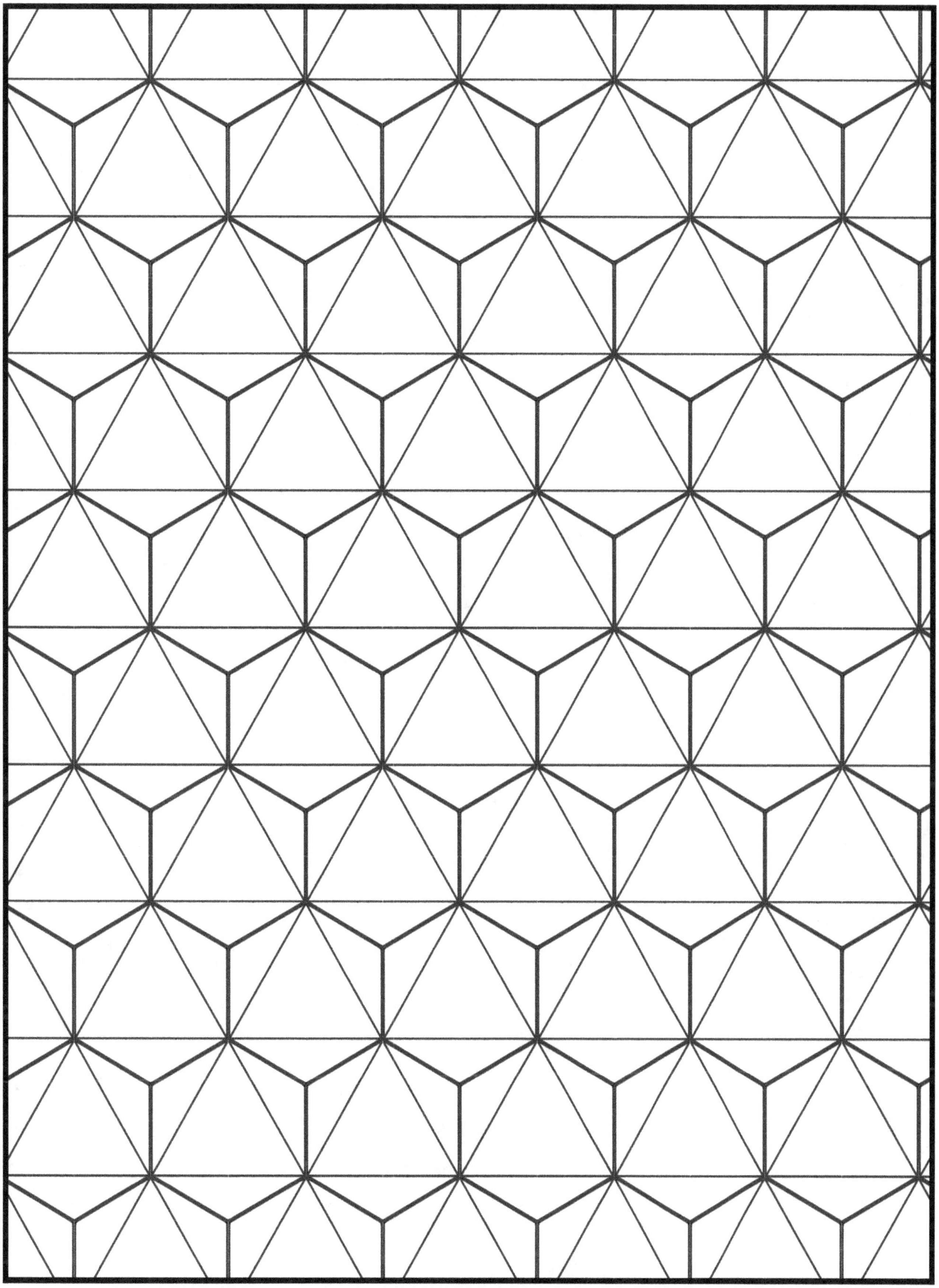

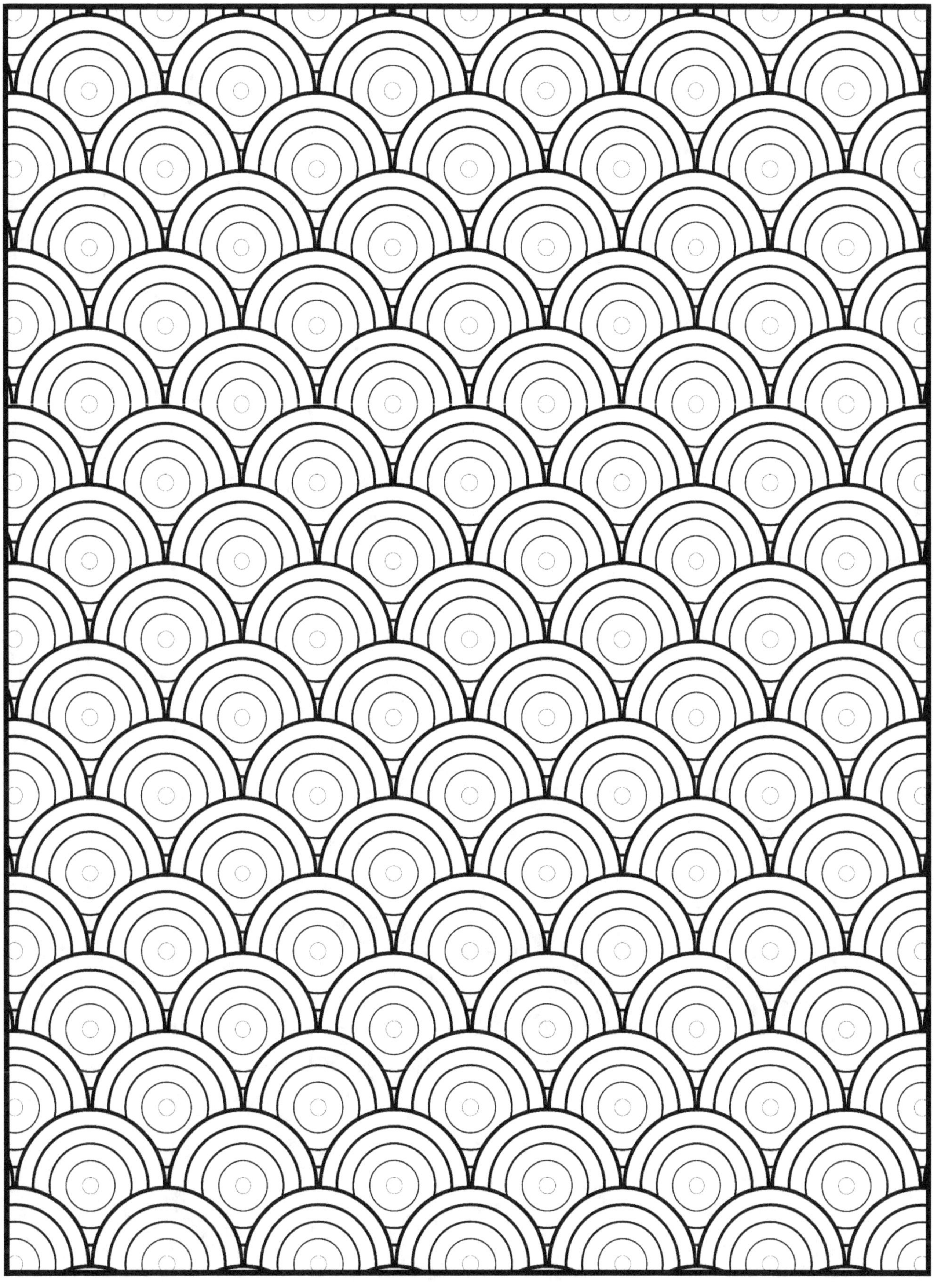

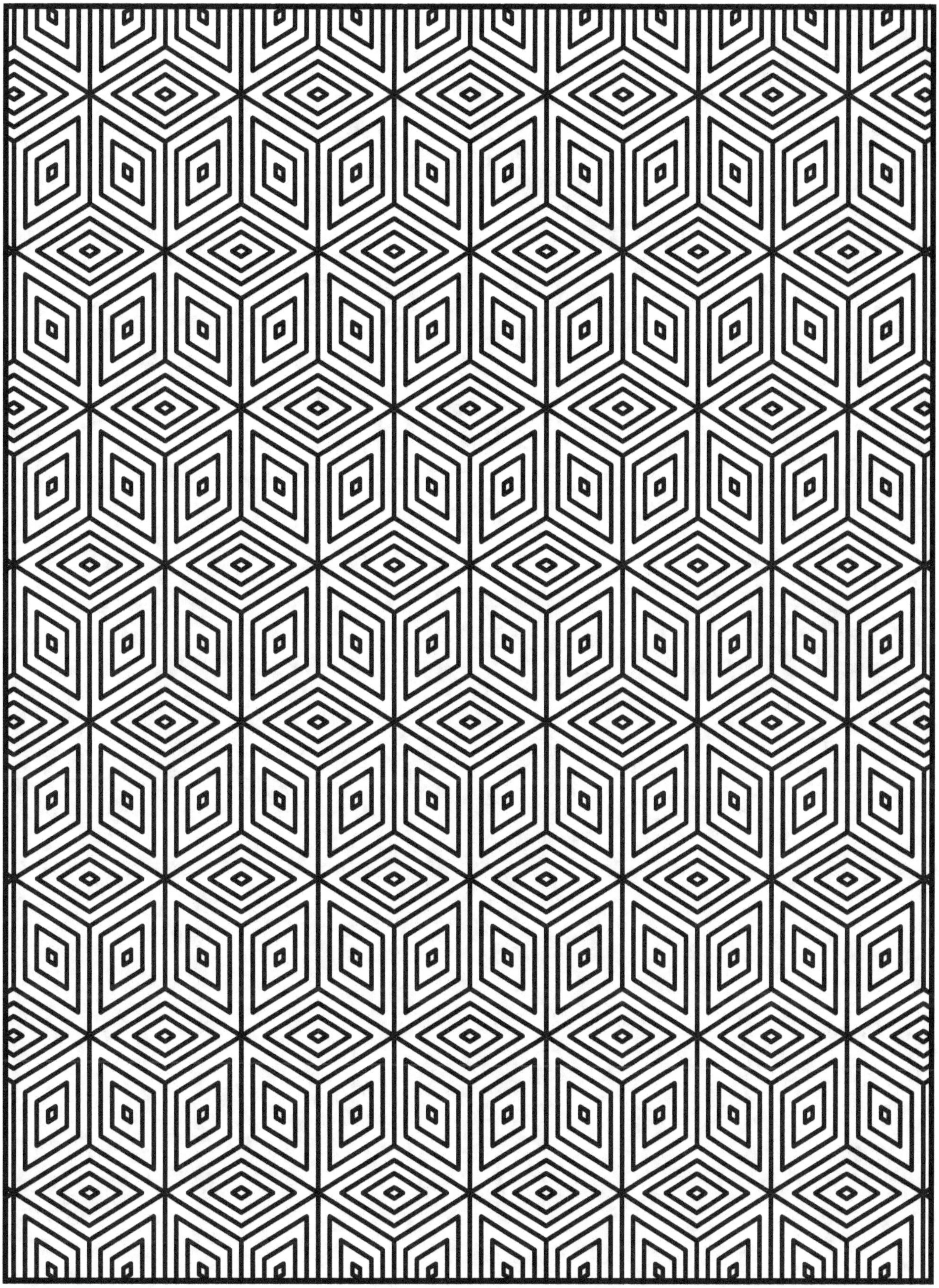

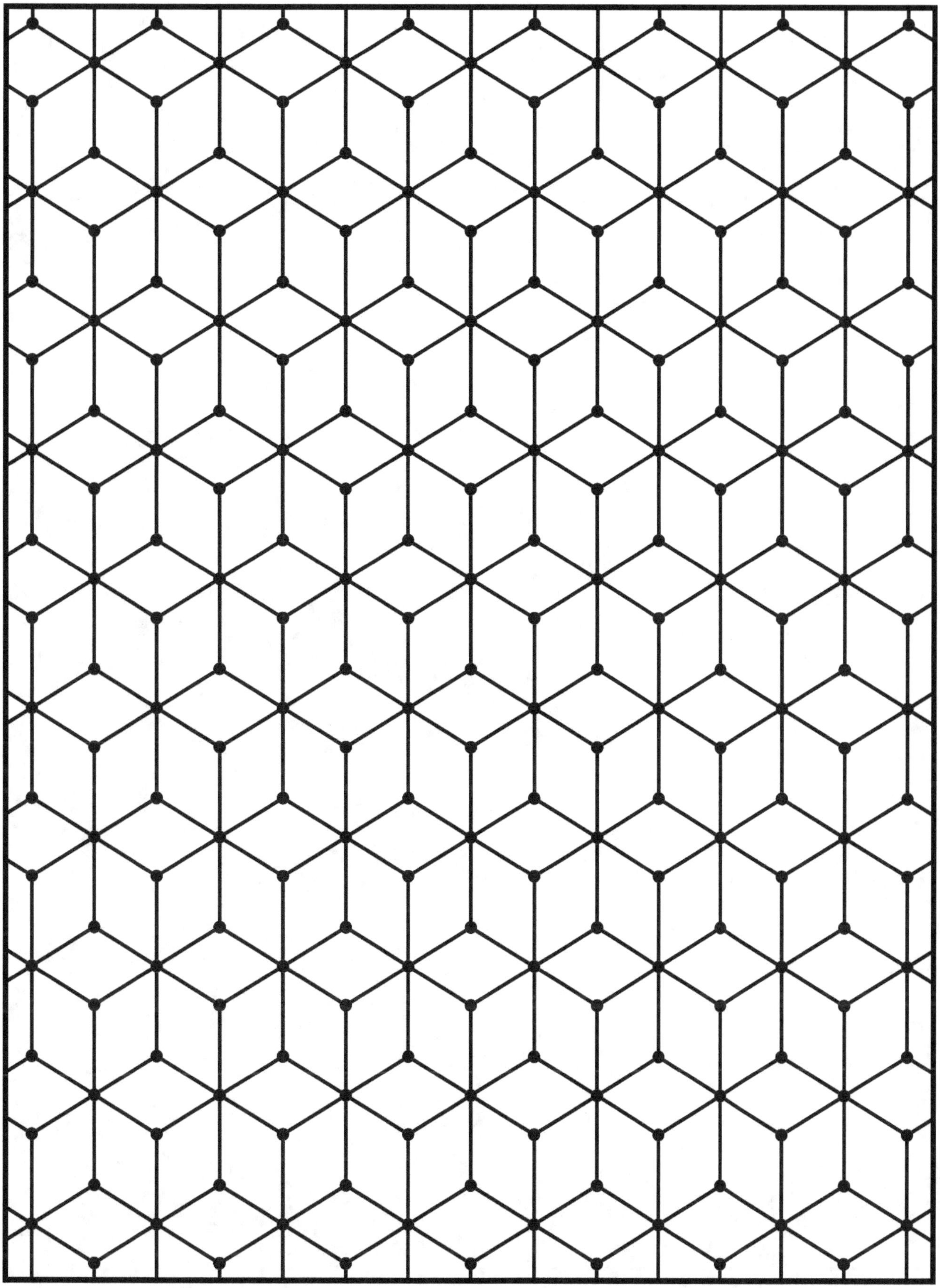

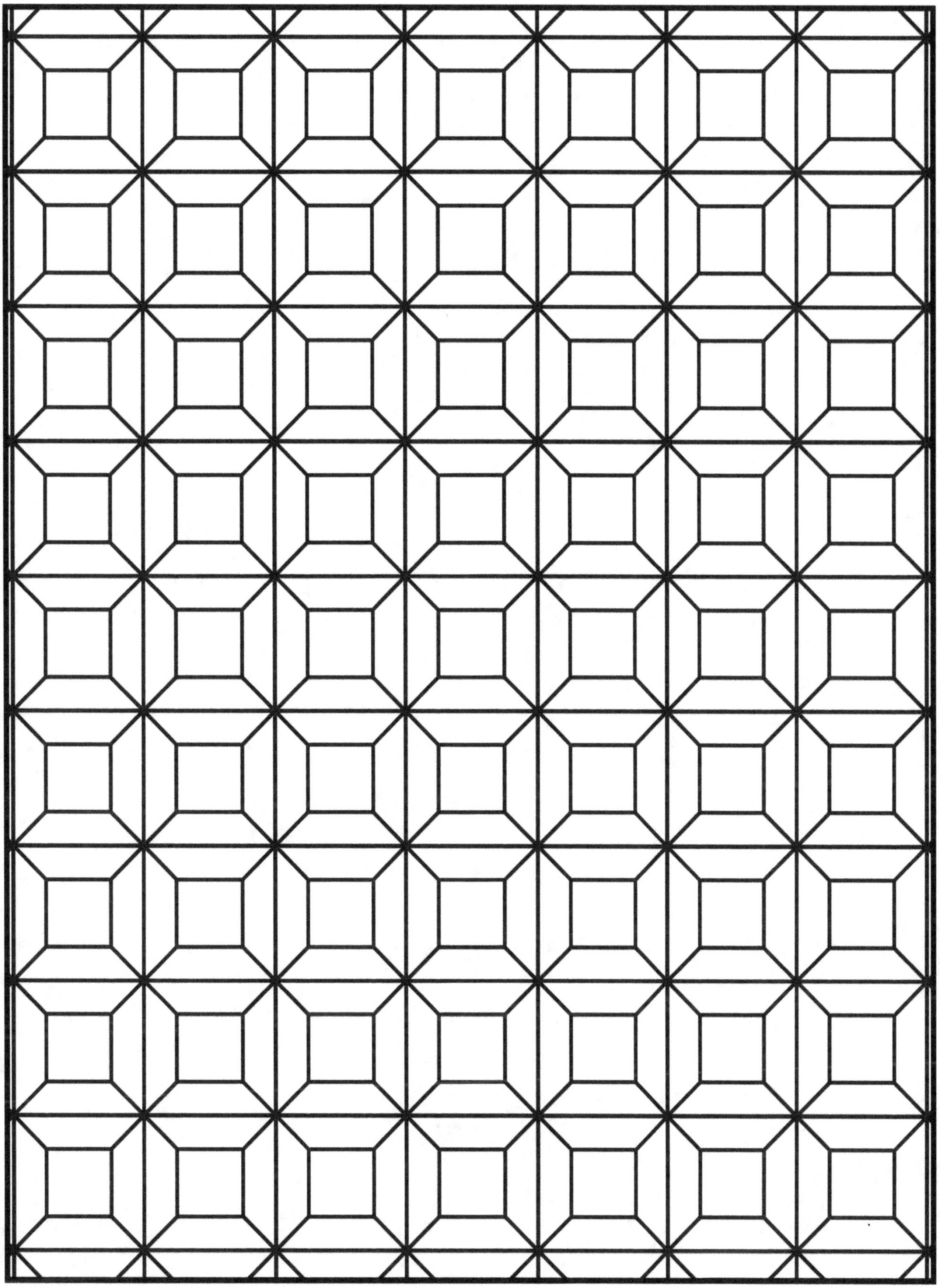

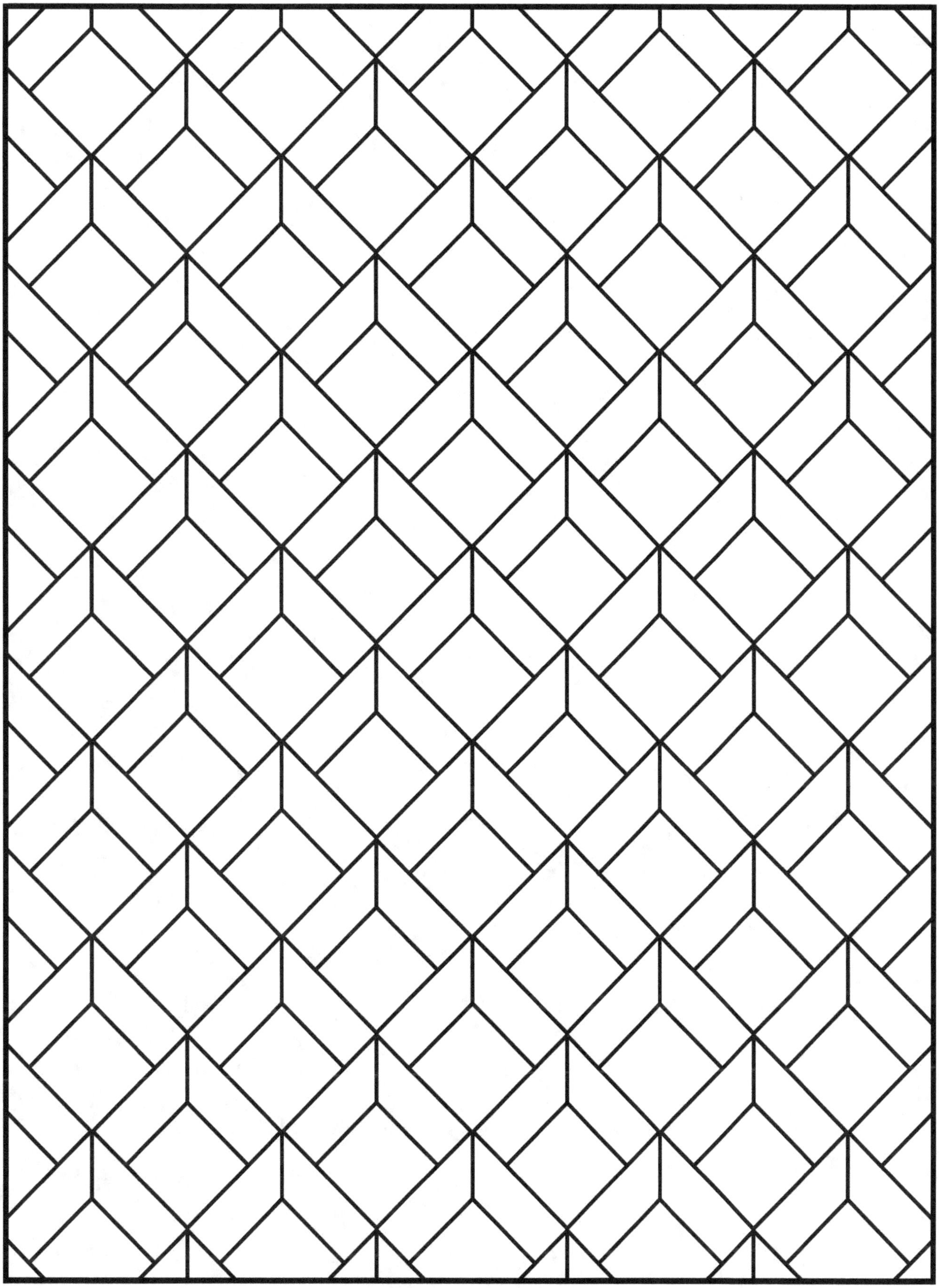

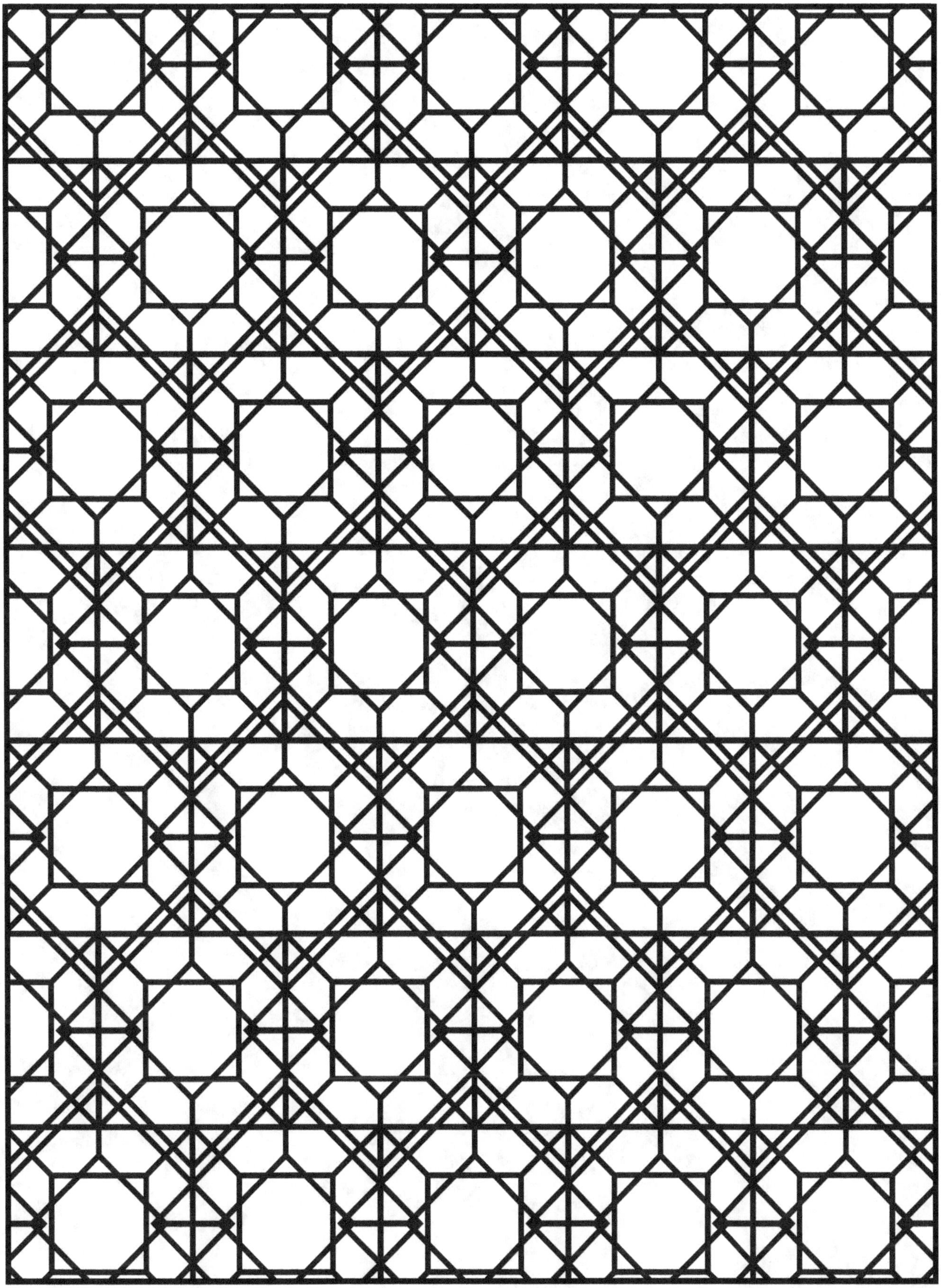

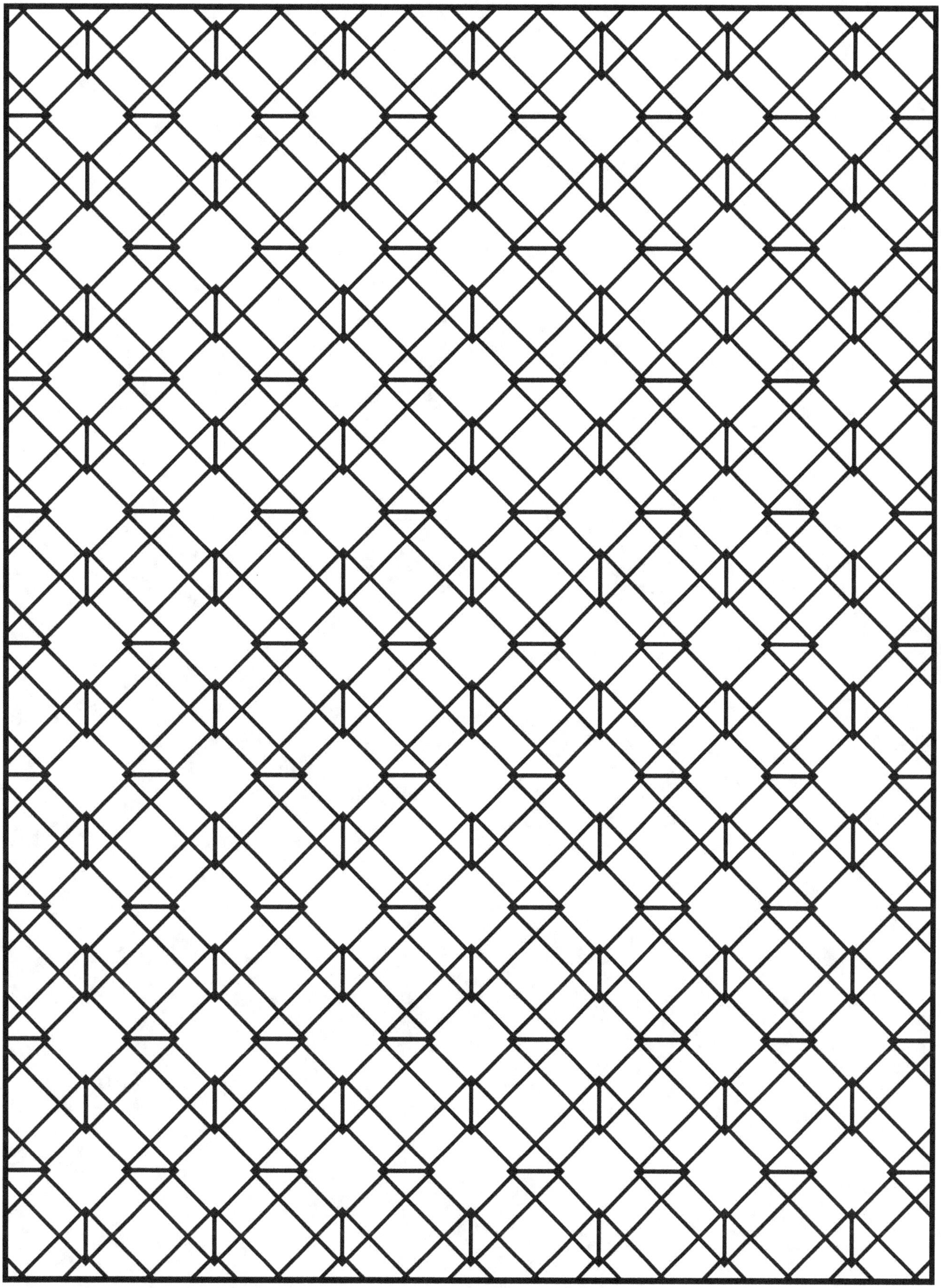

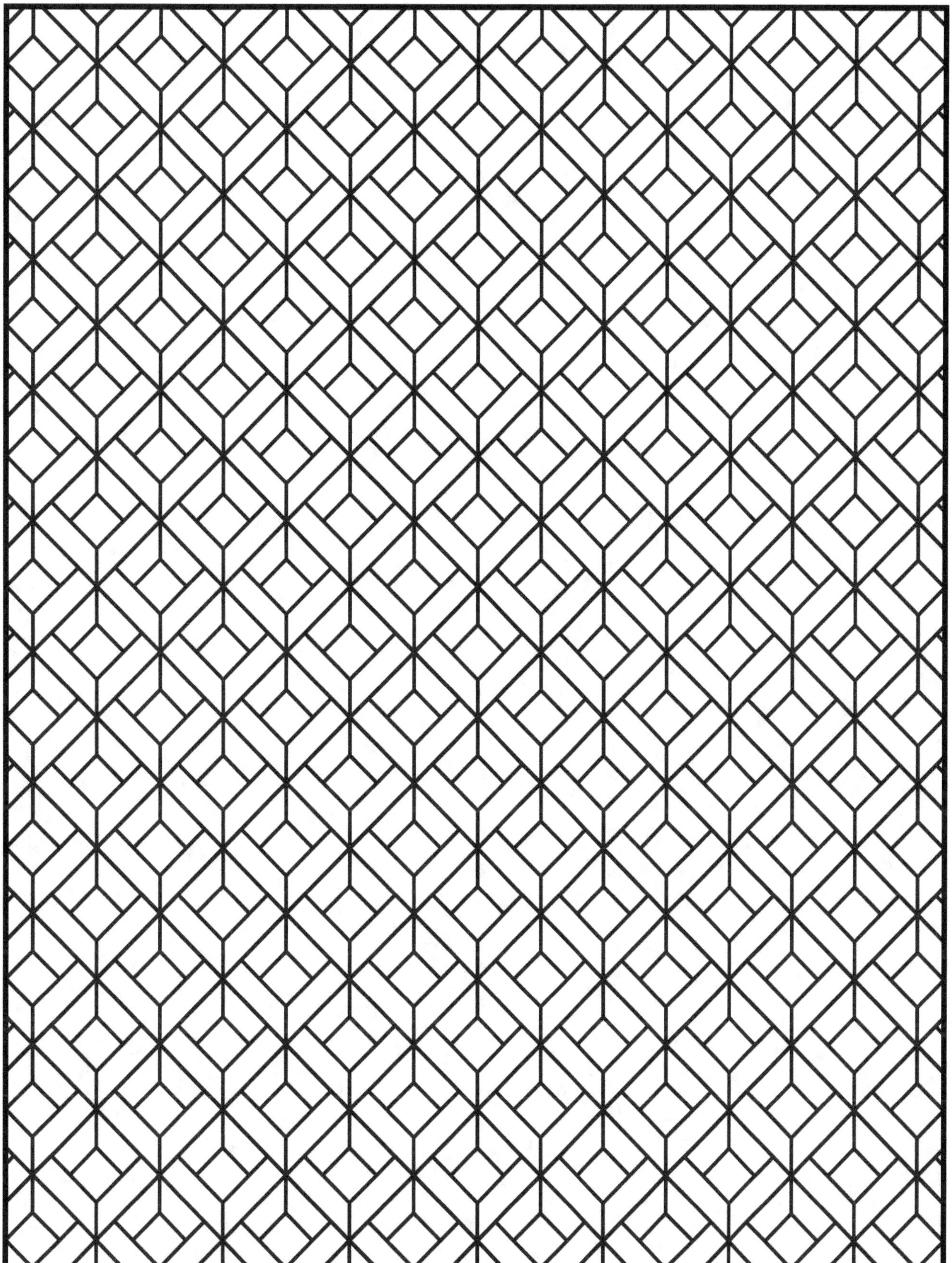

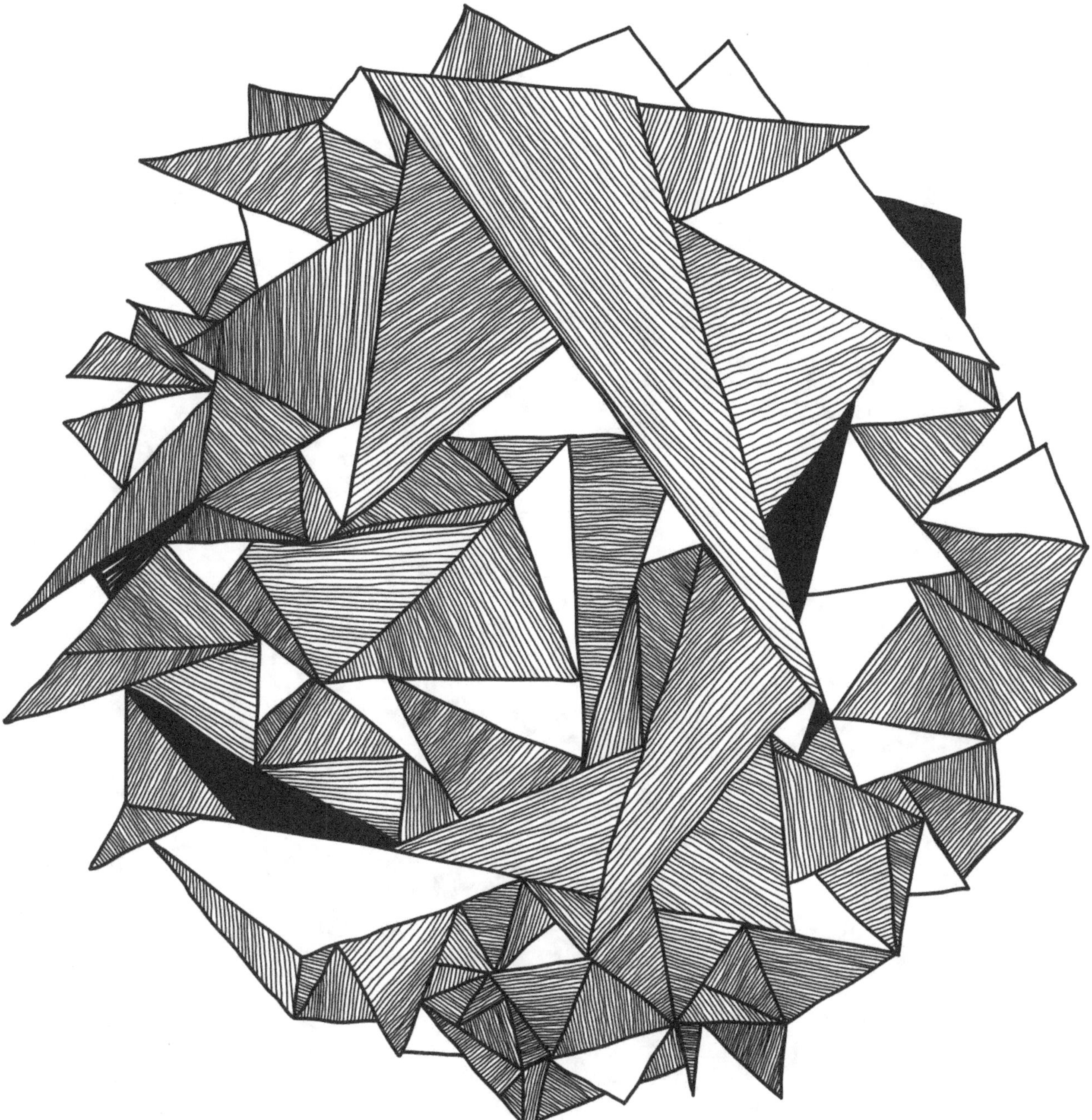

www.ingramcontent.com/pod-product-compliance
Lightning Source LLC
Chambersburg PA
CBHW081557170526
45166CB00009B/2732
* 9 7 8 1 5 2 2 8 0 0 2 6 2 *